Learning from Failure

Keys to Success

Gerard Assey

Learning from Failure

Keys to Success

By

Gerard Assey

Published by:

Gerard Assey

19/18, Palli Arasan Street

Anna Nagar East

Chennai - 600 102

ISBN: 978-81-972591-8-0

(Image courtesy Freepik: www.Freepik.com-Thank You)

Table of Contents

Preface

In a world that often glorifies success and shuns failure, it is easy to overlook the profound lessons embedded in our setbacks. Yet, it is precisely through failure that we learn the most about ourselves, our capabilities, and the paths we need to take to achieve true success. This book, **"Learning from Failure: *Keys to Success,*"** is born out of the conviction that every failure carries the seed of a valuable lesson and the potential for personal growth.

My own journey has been marked by numerous failures, each one a stepping stone that guided me toward greater understanding and resilience. It is these experiences that have shaped my perspective and inspired me to share the insights I have gained with you. This book is not merely a collection of theories but a practical guide grounded in real-life examples, actionable plans, and interactive elements designed to engage and empower you.

The chapters of this book are structured to take you on a transformative journey. Starting with a deep dive into understanding failure, you will learn to reframe setbacks as opportunities for growth. You will then be guided through the process of analyzing your failures, building resilience, and setting new, achievable goals. Each chapter is filled with practical tools and resources, including templates, worksheets, and checklists, to help you implement the strategies discussed.

One of the unique features of this book is its emphasis on interactive elements. At the end of each chapter, you will find reflective questions and journaling prompts designed to help you process your thoughts and track your progress. These prompts are not mere afterthoughts but integral parts of your learning journey, encouraging you to pause, reflect, and internalize the lessons.

Moreover, this book acknowledges the importance of support systems and mentorship. You will discover how to build a robust network of mentors and peers who can guide and inspire you. Through stories of resilience and adaptation, you will see how others have navigated their failures and emerged stronger.

As you progress through the chapters, you will learn to celebrate your successes, no matter how small, and use them as fuel to sustain your momentum. Finally, you will be encouraged to share your story and give back by mentoring others, creating a legacy of resilience and success.

"Learning from Failure: *Keys to Success*" is more than just a book; it is a companion on your journey to personal and professional growth. It is my hope that through the exercises, action plans, and reflections, you will discover the strength within you to embrace failure, learn from it, and ultimately achieve the success you deserve.

Thank you for allowing me to be a part of your journey. May this book be a source of inspiration and a guide as you navigate the complexities of failure and success.

Understanding Failure

Introduction to Failure

Failure. The word itself often conjures images of disappointment, missed opportunities, and personal shortcomings. For many, failure is a taboo topic, something to be avoided at all costs. Society tends to glorify success while sweeping failures under the rug. Yet, failure is an intrinsic part of the human experience. It is as natural as breathing and just as necessary for growth and progress.

To truly understand failure, we must first define it. Failure can be described as a lack of success in achieving a goal or objective. It is the opposite of success, but this binary view is overly simplistic and fails to capture the nuances of failure. Failure is not a permanent state but a temporary setback. It is an event, not a person. You may fail at a task, but you are not a failure.

Common perceptions of failure vary widely. Some see it as a devastating end, a confirmation of inadequacy, while others view it as a valuable learning experience. These differing perceptions can be shaped by personal beliefs, cultural influences, and past experiences. Historically, failure has been stigmatized, often linked to shame and embarrassment. However, modern perspectives are shifting towards a more constructive view, recognizing failure as a critical component of innovation and personal development.

Consider the historical example of Thomas Edison, who famously remarked, "I have not failed. I've just found 10,000 ways that won't work." Edison's numerous experiments and setbacks were stepping stones that led to the invention of the electric light bulb. Similarly, J.K. Rowling, before becoming a world-renowned author, faced numerous rejections from publishers. Her persistence in the face of failure eventually led to the creation of the beloved Harry Potter series. These examples illustrate that failure is not the end but a beginning, a catalyst for perseverance and eventual success.

The Role of Failure in Success

Why is failure such an integral part of the journey to success? The answer lies in the lessons it teaches and the resilience it builds. Failure forces us to confront our weaknesses, adapt our strategies, and try again with renewed vigor. It is a powerful teacher, providing insights that success alone cannot offer.

Failure teaches humility. It reminds us that we are not infallible and that perfection is a myth. This humility is crucial for personal growth, as it opens us to new ideas and perspectives. Failure also fosters resilience. The process of recovering from setbacks strengthens our resolve and enhances our ability to cope with future challenges. It is in these moments of adversity that our true character is revealed and forged.

Many famous success stories are born from failure. Take the case of Michael Jordan, widely regarded as one of the greatest basketball players of all time. He was cut from his high school basketball team, a moment that could have ended his career aspirations. Instead, it fueled his determination to succeed. Jordan's relentless work ethic and refusal to be defined by his failures led him to unparalleled success in the sport.

Another example is Oprah Winfrey, whose early career was marked by significant setbacks. She faced numerous personal and professional challenges, including being fired from her first television job. However, these failures did not deter her. They propelled her forward, ultimately leading her to become a media mogul and philanthropist. Winfrey's story underscores the idea that failure is not a roadblock but a detour, guiding us to new paths and opportunities.

Action Plan: Reframing Failure

To harness the power of failure, we must learn to reframe our mindset. This involves changing our perception of failure from a negative outcome to a positive, growth-oriented experience. Here are some exercises and steps to help you view failures as learning opportunities:

- ✓ **Practice Self-Compassion:** When you experience failure, treat yourself with kindness and understanding. Acknowledge your efforts and remind yourself that failure is a part of the learning process. Self-compassion can mitigate the negative emotions associated with failure and promote a healthier, more constructive response.
- ✓ **Reflect on Your Experience:** Take time to analyze what went wrong. Reflect on the situation, your actions, and the outcome. Ask yourself questions like, "What can I learn from this?" and "How can I improve next time?" Reflection turns failure into a valuable learning tool, providing insights that can guide future efforts.
- ✓ **Embrace a Growth Mindset:** Adopt the belief that your abilities and intelligence can be developed through dedication and hard work. A growth mindset fosters a love for learning

and resilience in the face of challenges. It helps you see failure as a stepping stone rather than a stumbling block.

- ✓ **Set Realistic Goals:** Sometimes, failure occurs because our goals are unrealistic or too ambitious. Break your larger goals into smaller, manageable steps. Celebrate small wins along the way, and adjust your goals as needed based on your progress and learnings.
- ✓ **Seek Feedback:** Constructive feedback from others can provide valuable perspectives on your failures. Seek input from trusted mentors, peers, or coaches. Use their insights to identify areas for improvement and to develop new strategies.
- ✓ **Keep a Failure Journal:** Document your failures and the lessons you've learned from them. Writing about your experiences can provide clarity and help you track your growth over time. It also serves as a reminder that failure is a natural part of your journey.

By reframing failure, you can transform it from a source of fear and frustration into a powerful tool for growth and success. Embrace failure, learn from it, and let it propel you towards your goals. Remember, every failure is an opportunity to begin again, this time with greater wisdom and determination.

Reflective Questions:

- ✓ How do you currently define failure, and how has your definition changed over time?

- ✓ Can you recall a significant failure in your life? What were your initial feelings and reactions to this failure?
- ✓ How have your perceptions of failure influenced your decisions and actions in the past?
- ✓ How do you think embracing failure could change your approach to challenges?

Journaling Prompts:

- ✓ Describe a recent failure and how it made you feel. What did you learn from this experience?
- ✓ Write about a historical or modern figure who experienced failure before achieving success. How did their journey inspire you?
- ✓ Reflect on a time when you feared failure. What was the outcome, and what did you learn about yourself?
- ✓ How can you reframe your mindset to view failures as learning opportunities rather than setbacks?

Analyzing Your Failures

Failure is not just an event but an opportunity for growth and learning. The first step towards leveraging failure for success is to analyze it thoroughly. This process begins with reflection and moves into a structured analysis to uncover the root causes. By understanding why you failed, you can develop actionable steps to avoid repeating the same mistakes and to improve your strategies for future success.

Reflecting on Your Experiences

Self-reflection is a critical component of personal development, especially when it comes to understanding failure. Reflecting on your experiences allows you to gain insights into your actions, thoughts, and emotions, providing a clearer picture of what went wrong and why. It's through this introspection that you can begin to identify patterns, recognize mistakes, and understand the underlying factors that contributed to your failure.

The Importance of Self-Reflection in Understanding Failure

Self-reflection is more than just thinking about what happened. It's a deliberate process of examining your experiences, behaviors, and outcomes to learn from them. When you reflect on your failures, you give yourself the chance to:

- ✓ Gain Clarity: Understand the sequence of events that led to the failure.
- ✓ Identify Emotions: Recognize the emotional responses that influenced your decisions.

- ✓ Recognize Patterns: Spot recurring behaviors or choices that may contribute to repeated failures.
- ✓ Learn from Mistakes: Extract valuable lessons that can inform future actions and decisions.

Reflecting on your failures helps you move beyond the surface-level reasons for your setbacks and delve into the deeper causes. It allows you to see the bigger picture and understand the complex interplay of factors that led to the failure.

Techniques for Effective Reflection

Effective reflection requires time, effort, and a structured approach. Here are two powerful techniques that can aid in this process:

1. Journaling: Writing about your experiences is one of the most effective ways to reflect. Journaling allows you to organize your thoughts, explore your emotions, and articulate the lessons you've learned. When journaling about a failure, consider the following prompts:

- ✓ Describe the event in detail. What happened?
- ✓ How did you feel during and after the event?
- ✓ What factors contributed to the failure?
- ✓ What could you have done differently?
- ✓ What have you learned from this experience?

2. Meditation: Meditation helps calm the mind and allows you to focus on your thoughts and feelings without judgment. A specific type of meditation called "mindfulness meditation" can be particularly useful. This involves sitting quietly, focusing on your breath, and gently bringing your attention to your thoughts and feelings about the failure. By observing these thoughts without attachment, you can gain insights and achieve a more balanced perspective.

Identifying Root Causes

Once you have reflected on your failure, the next step is to analyze it systematically to identify the root causes. This process involves moving beyond the obvious reasons and uncovering the deeper, often hidden factors that contributed to the failure.

Tools for Root Cause Analysis

Several tools can help you perform a thorough root cause analysis. Two of the most effective are the Fishbone Diagram and the 5 Whys technique.

1. Fishbone Diagram: Also known as the Ishikawa or cause-and-effect diagram, this tool helps you visually map out the potential causes of a problem. To create a Fishbone Diagram:

- ✓ Write the problem or failure at the head of the fish.
- ✓ Draw a straight line (the spine) from the head.
- ✓ Identify major categories of causes (e.g., people, processes, materials, environment) and draw branches off the spine for each category.
- ✓ For each category, brainstorm possible causes and add them as smaller branches off the main branches.
- ✓ Continue to break down each cause into more specific factors until you reach the root causes.

2. 5 Whys: This technique involves asking "why" repeatedly (usually five times) to drill down into the underlying causes of a problem. Here's how to use the 5 Whys:

- ✓ Start with the problem statement.
- ✓ Ask "Why did this happen?" and write down the answer.
- ✓ Take the answer and ask "Why?" again.

- ✓ Repeat this process until you have asked "Why?" five times or until you reach a fundamental cause that cannot be broken down further.

Case Studies of Failure Analysis in Different Contexts

To illustrate how these tools work in practice, let's look at two case studies:

1. Startup Failure:

Problem: A tech startup failed to secure a second round of funding.

Fishbone Diagram: The team identified potential causes such as poor market research, inadequate product features, weak marketing strategy, and insufficient investor relations.

5 Whys:

- ✓ Why did we fail to secure funding? Because our product did not meet investor expectations.
- ✓ Why did our product not meet expectations? Because it lacked key features.
- ✓ Why did it lack key features? Because our market research was inadequate.
- ✓ Why was our market research inadequate? Because we did not allocate enough resources to it.
- ✓ Why did we not allocate enough resources? Because we underestimated the importance of market research.

2. Personal Project Failure:

Problem: An individual failed to complete a marathon.

Fishbone Diagram: The person identified causes such as lack of training, poor nutrition, inadequate rest, and mental preparation.

5 Whys:

- ✓ Why did I fail to complete the marathon? Because I was exhausted halfway through.
- ✓ Why was I exhausted? Because I did not train adequately.
- ✓ Why did I not train adequately? Because I had a busy work schedule.
- ✓ Why did my work schedule interfere with training? Because I did not prioritize my training.
- ✓ Why did I not prioritize training? Because I did not set clear goals and manage my time effectively.

Action Plan: Conducting a Failure Analysis

Conducting a failure analysis involves a structured approach to ensure that you gain the maximum insights from your experience. Here is a step-by-step guide to help you through the process:

1. Document the Failure:
   - ✓ Write a detailed account of the failure. Include what happened, when it happened, who was involved, and the immediate outcomes.
   - ✓ Be honest and objective in your description. Avoid assigning blame and focus on the facts.
2. Reflect on Your Experience:
   - ✓ Use journaling or meditation to explore your thoughts and feelings about the failure.
   - ✓ Identify any emotional responses that may have influenced your actions and decisions.
3. Create a Fishbone Diagram:
   - ✓ Write down the failure at the head of the fish.
   - ✓ Identify the main categories of potential causes and draw them as branches off the spine.

- ✓ Brainstorm and add specific causes for each category. Break them down into smaller factors until you identify the root causes.

4. Perform the 5 Whys Analysis:
   - ✓ Starting with the failure, ask "Why?" to uncover the underlying causes.
   - ✓ Continue asking "Why?" for each answer until you reach a fundamental cause.
5. Summarize Your Findings:
   - ✓ Review the results of your Fishbone Diagram and 5 Whys analysis.
   - ✓ Identify the key root causes of the failure and document them.
6. Create an Action List:
   - ✓ Based on your findings, develop a list of actionable steps to address the root causes.
   - ✓ Prioritize these actions and set specific, measurable goals for each one.
   - ✓ Include deadlines and assign responsibilities if applicable.
7. Implement and Monitor:
   - ✓ Take action on your plan and monitor your progress.
   - ✓ Regularly review your action list and adjust as needed based on new insights and developments.

Example Action List:

Root Cause: Inadequate market research (Startup Failure)

- ✓ Action: Allocate additional resources to market research.
- ✓ Goal: Conduct comprehensive market research within the next three months.
- ✓ Deadline: August 31, 2024.

- ✓ Responsibility: Assign a dedicated team member to lead the research effort.

Root Cause: Lack of training (Marathon Failure)

- ✓ Action: Develop a detailed training plan.
- ✓ Goal: Follow a structured training schedule for six months.
- ✓ Deadline: November 30, 2024.
- ✓ Responsibility: Create a training calendar and track progress weekly.

By following this structured approach to failure analysis, you can gain valuable insights, develop effective strategies for improvement, and ultimately turn your failures into stepping stones for success. Remember, failure is not the end but a powerful beginning, a chance to learn, grow, and achieve greater heights.

Reflective Questions:

- ✓ What methods have you used in the past to reflect on your failures? Were they effective?
- ✓ Can you identify any patterns or recurring themes in your past failures?
- ✓ How do you distinguish between a failure caused by external factors and one caused by internal factors?
- ✓ What are the root causes of your most recent failure, and how did you identify them?

Journaling Prompts:

- ✓ Write about a failure that taught you a valuable lesson. What was the lesson, and how did you learn it?
- ✓ Use a fishbone diagram or the 5 Whys method to analyze a specific failure. What did you discover about the root causes?

- ✓ Reflect on a failure in a professional context. What steps did you take to analyze and understand this failure?
- ✓ How can you apply the lessons learned from past failures to future challenges?

Building Resilience

Failure is an inevitable part of life, but how we respond to it can make all the difference. This is where resilience comes in. Resilience is the ability to bounce back from setbacks, adapt to adversity, and keep moving forward despite the challenges. In this chapter, we will explore the nature of resilience, how to develop a resilient mindset, and practical action plans to strengthen your resilience.

The Nature of Resilience

Resilience is often described as the capacity to recover quickly from difficulties. It is the mental and emotional fortitude that helps us navigate life's ups and downs. While some people seem naturally resilient, resilience is not an innate trait but a skill that can be developed over time.

What Resilience Is and Why It's Crucial

Resilience involves a combination of behaviors, thoughts, and actions that can be learned and cultivated. It is about being able to endure hardships and emerge stronger. Resilience is crucial because it:

- ✓ Promotes Well-Being: Resilient individuals are better able to manage stress and maintain a positive outlook, which contributes to overall mental and emotional health.
- ✓ Enhances Performance: In the face of challenges, resilient people can stay focused and perform effectively, whether in their personal lives or professional careers.
- ✓ Supports Adaptability: Resilience allows individuals to adapt to changing

- ✓ circumstances and find new ways to approach problems.
- ✓ Fosters Growth: By overcoming adversity, resilient individuals learn valuable lessons and grow from their experiences.

Psychological and Emotional Aspects of Resilience

Resilience is deeply rooted in psychological and emotional processes. It involves regulating emotions, maintaining a sense of control, and staying motivated even when things go wrong. Key aspects include:

- ✓ Emotional Regulation: The ability to manage and respond to intense emotions in a healthy way. This includes recognizing and accepting emotions rather than suppressing them.
- ✓ Self-Efficacy: Belief in one's ability to influence events and outcomes. This confidence helps individuals take proactive steps to solve problems and overcome challenges.
- ✓ Optimism: Maintaining a hopeful outlook and expecting positive outcomes. Optimism is not about ignoring reality but about seeing possibilities even in difficult situations.
- ✓ Social Support: Building strong, supportive relationships that provide comfort, advice, and encouragement during tough times.

Developing a Resilient Mindset

Building resilience starts with cultivating a resilient mindset. This involves changing how you think about adversity and developing mental toughness.

Strategies to Build Mental Toughness

- ✓ Positive Self-Talk: The way you talk to yourself can significantly impact your resilience. Positive self-talk involves replacing negative thoughts with positive affirmations.

For instance, instead of thinking, "I can't handle this," tell yourself, "I am capable of overcoming this challenge."

- ✓ Growth Mindset: Embrace the belief that your abilities and intelligence can be developed through effort and learning. A growth mindset encourages you to see failures as opportunities to grow rather than insurmountable obstacles. Carol Dweck's research on mindset highlights how individuals with a growth mindset are more resilient in the face of adversity.
- ✓ Goal Setting: Set realistic and achievable goals. Break down larger goals into smaller, manageable steps. This helps you maintain focus and motivation, making it easier to navigate setbacks along the way.

Stories of Resilient Individuals

To understand the power of resilience, let's look at some inspirational stories:

- ✓ Nelson Mandela: Mandela's life is a testament to resilience. Despite spending 27 years in prison under harsh conditions, he emerged with a vision of reconciliation and unity for South Africa. His resilience not only helped him survive but also led to profound social and political change in his country.
- ✓ Malala Yousafzai: Malala's story is another powerful example. After being shot by the Taliban for advocating girls' education, she continued her activism with even more determination. Her resilience has made her a global symbol of courage and the fight for education rights.

Action Plan: Strengthening Resilience

Building resilience requires consistent effort and the integration of various practices into your daily life. Here's how you can strengthen your resilience through practical steps.

Daily Practices to Enhance Resilience

- ✓ Exercise: Regular physical activity is not only good for your body but also for your mind. Exercise releases endorphins, which help reduce stress and improve mood. Aim for at least 30 minutes of moderate exercise most days of the week.
- ✓ Mindfulness and Meditation: Practicing mindfulness helps you stay present and manage stress. Meditation can increase emotional regulation and reduce anxiety. Start with just a few minutes each day, focusing on your breath and observing your thoughts without judgment.
- ✓ Healthy Routine: Maintain a balanced diet, get adequate sleep, and ensure you have a routine that includes time for relaxation and hobbies. A healthy body supports a resilient mind.

Long-Term Resilience-Building Activities

- ✓ Develop Strong Relationships: Build and nurture a support network of family, friends, and colleagues. Having people to turn to during difficult times provides emotional support and practical advice.
- ✓ Continuous Learning: Commit to lifelong learning and personal development. Engage in activities that challenge you and expand your skills and knowledge. This could include taking courses, reading books, or engaging in new hobbies.

- ✓ Volunteer and Help Others: Helping others can boost your resilience by giving you a sense of purpose and perspective. Volunteering connects you with your community and allows you to contribute positively, which can enhance your own well-being.

Example Action Plan for Building Resilience

- ✓ Daily Journaling: Spend 10 minutes each evening writing about your day. Focus on what went well, what challenges you faced, and how you responded to them. Reflect on how you can apply these insights to future situations.
- ✓ Weekly Reflection: At the end of each week, review your journal entries. Identify any recurring patterns or triggers that affect your resilience. Set goals for the upcoming week to address these areas.
- ✓ Monthly Goal Setting: Set specific, achievable goals for each month. Break these goals into smaller tasks and track your progress. Celebrate your successes and learn from any setbacks.
- ✓ Social Engagement: Schedule regular time with friends and family. Plan activities that you enjoy and that allow you to build stronger connections. Make an effort to reach out and offer support to others in your network.
- ✓ Learning and Growth: Choose a new skill or subject to learn each quarter. Dedicate time each week to studying and practicing this new skill. Reflect on how this learning experience contributes to your personal and professional growth.

By incorporating these practices into your daily routine, you can build a resilient mindset and develop the emotional and psychological tools needed to navigate life's challenges. Remember, resilience is not about avoiding failure but about facing it head-on, learning from it, and growing stronger as a result.

Reflective Questions:

- ✓ How do you currently define resilience, and why do you think it's important?
- ✓ Describe a situation where you demonstrated resilience. What factors helped you bounce back?
- ✓ What psychological and emotional strategies have you used to build resilience?
- ✓ How can you strengthen your resilience in areas where you feel it is lacking?

Journaling Prompts:

- ✓ Write about a time when you faced a significant challenge. How did you cope, and what helped you persevere?
- ✓ Reflect on the story of Nelson Mandela or Malala Yousafzai. What aspects of their resilience can you incorporate into your own life?
- ✓ List the daily practices you can start to enhance your resilience. How will you integrate these into your routine?
- ✓ How does maintaining a positive self-talk influence your resilience in difficult situations?

Setting New Goals

Setting new goals after experiencing failure is an essential step in the journey towards success. Goals provide a sense of direction, motivation, and a roadmap to guide our actions. This chapter delves into the importance of goal setting, how to revise goals after failure, and practical steps to create effective goals.

The Importance of Goal Setting

Goals are the milestones that mark our journey toward achieving our aspirations. They are the benchmarks against which we measure progress and success. Without goals, we can easily lose our way, lack motivation, and struggle to find purpose in our actions.

How Goals Provide Direction and Motivation

Setting goals helps to clarify what we want to achieve and the steps needed to get there. Goals provide a clear direction, helping us to focus our efforts and resources on what truly matters. They act as a compass, guiding us through the challenges and uncertainties that we encounter along the way.

Moreover, goals are powerful motivators. They give us something to strive for and a reason to keep pushing forward, even when the going gets tough. When we set and achieve goals, we experience a sense of accomplishment that boosts our confidence and drives us to set and pursue even higher aspirations.

SMART Goals and Their Effectiveness

One of the most effective ways to set goals is by using the SMART criteria. SMART goals are Specific, Measurable, Achievable, Relevant, and Time-bound.

This framework ensures that goals are clear, realistic, and trackable, increasing the likelihood of success.

- ✓ Specific: A specific goal clearly defines what you want to achieve. Instead of setting a vague goal like "I want to get fit," a specific goal would be "I want to run a 5K race in three months."
- ✓ Measurable: A measurable goal includes criteria to track progress. For example, "I will track my running distance and time each week."
- ✓ Achievable: An achievable goal is realistic and attainable given your current resources and constraints. It challenges you but is still possible.
- ✓ Relevant: A relevant goal aligns with your broader objectives and values. It should matter to you and contribute to your overall purpose.
- ✓ Time-bound: A time-bound goal has a deadline, creating a sense of urgency and helping to prioritize tasks. For example, "I will complete my 5K training program in 12 weeks."

Revising Your Goals After Failure

Experiencing failure does not mean abandoning your goals. Instead, it provides an opportunity to reassess and revise them. Failure can offer valuable insights into what went wrong and how to improve your approach.

Techniques for Setting Realistic and Attainable Goals Post-Failure

- ✓ Reflect on Past Failures: Take time to analyze why you failed to achieve your previous goals.

Was it due to unrealistic expectations, lack of resources, or unforeseen obstacles? Understanding the root causes will help you set more realistic goals.

- ✓ Adjust Your Expectations: After a failure, it is important to set goals that are challenging but achievable. Adjust your expectations to match your current situation and capabilities.
- ✓ Break Down Large Goals: Large, ambitious goals can be overwhelming. Break them down into smaller, manageable steps. This approach allows you to achieve quick wins, maintain momentum, and build confidence.
- ✓ Seek Feedback and Support: Don't be afraid to ask for feedback from mentors, peers, or professionals. They can provide valuable insights and help you refine your goals. Additionally, having a support system can keep you motivated and accountable.

Examples of Successful Goal Re-Setting

- ✓ Case Study 1: Thomas Edison Thomas Edison, the famous inventor, faced numerous failures before successfully inventing the electric light bulb. After each failure, Edison did not give up. Instead, he analyzed what went wrong, adjusted his approach, and set new, attainable goals. His resilience and ability to revise his goals ultimately led to one of the most significant inventions in history.
- ✓ Case Study 2: Oprah Winfrey Oprah Winfrey faced multiple setbacks early in her career, including being fired from her job as a news anchor. Instead of giving up, she reassessed her goals and pursued opportunities that aligned with her passion for storytelling and

connecting with people. By revising her goals and leveraging her strengths, Oprah built a media empire and became one of the most influential figures in the world.

Action Plan: Goal Setting Workshop

Setting new goals requires a structured approach to ensure they are effective and achievable. This action plan provides a step-by-step guide and practical tools to help you set and track your goals.

Step-by-Step Guide to Setting and Tracking New Goals

- ✓ Identify Your Objectives: Start by identifying what you want to achieve. Consider both short-term and long-term goals. Write down your objectives and ensure they align with your values and overall purpose.
- ✓ Define Your Goals Using SMART Criteria: For each objective, create SMART goals. Make them specific, measurable, achievable, relevant, and time-bound.
- ✓ Develop an Action Plan: Break down each goal into smaller tasks or steps. Create a timeline for each task and set deadlines. This will help you stay organized and focused.
- ✓ Track Your Progress: Regularly monitor your progress towards your goals. Use tools like journals, spreadsheets, or goal-tracking apps to record your achievements and identify areas for improvement.
- ✓ Adjust as Needed: Be flexible and willing to adjust your goals as circumstances change. If you encounter obstacles, reassess and revise your goals to ensure they remain realistic and attainable.

Worksheets for Setting and Tracking New Goals

To assist you in setting and tracking your goals, use the following worksheets:

Goal Setting Worksheet

- ✓ Objective: ______________________________
- ✓ Specific Goal: ______________________________
- ✓ Measurable Criteria: ______________________________
- ✓ Achievable Steps: ______________________________
- ✓ Relevant Purpose: ______________________________
- ✓ Time-bound Deadline: ______________________________

Goal Tracking Worksheet

- ✓ Goal: ______________________________
- ✓ Steps/Tasks: ______________________________
- ✓ Start Date: ______________________________
- ✓ Completion Date: ______________________________
- ✓ Progress Notes: ______________________________

Tips for Maintaining Focus and Motivation

- ✓ Visualize Success: Regularly visualize yourself achieving your goals. This mental imagery can boost motivation and keep you focused.
- ✓ Celebrate Milestones: Celebrate your progress by acknowledging and rewarding

yourself for achieving milestones. This positive reinforcement can help maintain motivation.

- ✓ Stay Accountable: Share your goals with a friend, mentor, or support group. Regular check-ins can keep you accountable and provide encouragement.
- ✓ Stay Positive: Maintain a positive mindset and remind yourself of your capabilities and past successes. Positive self-talk can reinforce your commitment to your goals.

By following this action plan and using the provided worksheets, you can set new, realistic goals that propel you forward after experiencing failure. Remember, the key to success is not avoiding failure but learning from it and continuously striving towards your aspirations.

Reflective Questions:

- ✓ How do you feel when you achieve a goal? How do you feel when you fail to achieve a goal?
- ✓ What criteria do you use to set your goals? How do you ensure they are realistic and attainable?
- ✓ Reflect on a time when you had to revise your goals after a failure. What changes did you make, and what was the outcome?
- ✓ How do you stay motivated and focused on your goals, especially after experiencing a setback?

Journaling Prompts:

- ✓ Write about a goal you set and achieved. What steps did you take, and how did it feel to accomplish it?

- ✓ Reflect on a goal you didn't achieve. What factors contributed to this, and how can you adjust your approach next time?
- ✓ Use a SMART goal-setting worksheet to outline a new goal. Describe why this goal is important to you and how you plan to achieve it.
- ✓ How can you incorporate regular goal-setting and review sessions into your life to maintain progress and motivation?

Embracing a Growth Mindset

A growth mindset is the belief that abilities and intelligence can be developed through dedication, hard work, and continuous learning. In contrast, a fixed mindset assumes that talents and abilities are static traits that cannot be significantly changed. Understanding and embracing a growth mindset is essential for personal and professional growth, especially after experiencing failure. This chapter explores the differences between fixed and growth mindsets, practices for cultivating a growth mindset, and provides a detailed action plan to help you shift from a fixed to a growth mindset.

Fixed vs. Growth Mindset

Differences Between Fixed and Growth Mindsets

Carol Dweck, a psychologist and researcher at Stanford University, introduced the concepts of fixed and growth mindsets in her groundbreaking work. According to Dweck, individuals with a fixed mindset believe that their qualities are set in stone, which leads them to avoid challenges, give up easily, and feel threatened by the success of others. They often think statements like, "I'm just not good at this," or "I'll never be able to do that."

On the other hand, individuals with a growth mindset believe that their abilities and intelligence can be developed through effort, learning, and perseverance. They embrace challenges, persist in the face of setbacks, see effort as a path to mastery, and learn from criticism. They tend to think statements like, "I can improve with practice," or "Challenges help me grow."

The Impact of Mindset on Personal and Professional Growth

Your mindset profoundly impacts how you approach life's challenges and opportunities. A fixed mindset can lead to a fear of failure and a reluctance to try new things, limiting personal and professional growth. Conversely, a growth mindset fosters resilience, adaptability, and a continuous desire to learn and improve. This mindset shift can transform how you view failure—not as a reflection of your innate abilities but as a stepping stone towards growth and success.

Cultivating a Growth Mindset

Developing a growth mindset requires conscious effort and practice. Here are some effective strategies to help you cultivate this mindset.

Embracing Challenges

One of the hallmarks of a growth mindset is the willingness to embrace challenges. Rather than shying away from difficult tasks, see them as opportunities to learn and grow. When faced with a challenging situation, remind yourself that the effort you put in will lead to improvement and mastery. For example, if you are learning a new skill and find it difficult, instead of giving up, break the task into smaller steps and tackle each one with determination.

Learning from Criticism

Criticism can be hard to accept, especially when it feels personal. However, feedback is a valuable tool for growth. Instead of viewing criticism as a negative reflection of your abilities, see it as constructive input that can help you improve. For instance, if your manager provides feedback on a project, take notes on their suggestions and consider how you can implement these changes to enhance your performance. This approach transforms criticism into a learning opportunity.

Inspirational Quotes and Anecdotes

Inspiration can come from various sources, including quotes and stories of those who have embraced a growth mindset. Here are a few examples:

- ✓ **Thomas Edison:** Known for his perseverance, Edison famously said, *"I have not failed. I've just found 10,000 ways that won't work."* This quote highlights the importance of persistence and learning from every attempt.
- ✓ **Michael Jordan:** Widely regarded as one of the greatest basketball players of all time, Jordan once said, *"I've missed more than 9,000 shots in my career. I've lost almost 300 games. Twenty-six times, I've been trusted to take the game-winning shot and missed. I've failed over and over and over again in my life. And that is why I succeed."* His words emphasize that failure is a part of the journey to success.
- ✓ **J.K. Rowling:** Before finding success with the Harry Potter series, Rowling faced numerous rejections from publishers. She once remarked, *"It is impossible to live without failing at something, unless you live so cautiously that you might as well not have lived at all—in which case, you fail by default."* Her story is a testament to the power of persistence and believing in oneself.

Action Plan: Mindset Shift

To help you transition from a fixed to a growth mindset, here is a comprehensive action plan with exercises, reflection prompts, and affirmations.

Exercises to Shift from a Fixed to a Growth Mindset

- ✓ **Challenge Yourself:** Identify an area where you feel you are not naturally talented or have faced repeated failures. Set a small, achievable goal in this area and work towards it with determination. For example, if you struggle with public speaking, join a local Toastmasters club and practice giving short speeches.
- ✓ **Seek Feedback:** Choose a project or task you are currently working on and ask for feedback from a mentor, colleague, or friend. Listen to their suggestions with an open mind and use their input to make improvements.
- ✓ **Reflect on Setbacks:** Keep a journal where you document setbacks and failures. Write about what happened, how you felt, and what you learned from the experience. Reflect on how you can apply these lessons to future challenges.

Reflection Prompts and Affirmations

Reflection Prompts:

- ✓ Think about a recent challenge or failure you faced. How did you respond? What did you learn from the experience?
- ✓ Identify a time when you received constructive criticism. How did you react? How can you use this feedback to grow?
- ✓ Reflect on a skill or ability you believe is fixed. How can you approach this area with a growth mindset?

Affirmations:

- ✓ *"I embrace challenges and see them as opportunities to grow."*
- ✓ *"Feedback helps me improve and become better at what I do."*
- ✓ *"My abilities can be developed through hard work and dedication."*

Example Action Plan for Embracing a Growth Mindset

- ✓ **Daily Reflection:** Spend 10 minutes each evening reflecting on your day. Write about any challenges you faced and how you approached them. Consider what you learned and how you can apply these lessons moving forward.
- ✓ **Weekly Goal Setting:** Set a small, achievable goal each week that pushes you out of your comfort zone. At the end of the week, review your progress and adjust your goals as needed.
- ✓ **Monthly Feedback Session:** Schedule a monthly feedback session with a mentor or trusted colleague. Discuss your recent projects, seek their input, and create an action plan based on their suggestions.
- ✓ **Affirmation Practice:** Start each day by reciting growth mindset affirmations. This practice helps reinforce a positive outlook and sets the tone for your day.

By incorporating these practices into your daily routine, you can cultivate a growth mindset and transform how you approach challenges and setbacks. Remember, the key to success is not just about achieving your goals but also about developing the mindset that allows you to learn and grow from every experience.

Reflective Questions:

- ✓ How do you define a fixed mindset and a growth mindset? Which mindset do you tend to lean towards, and why?
- ✓ Describe a situation where having a growth mindset helped you overcome a challenge.
- ✓ What strategies have you used to cultivate a growth mindset, and how effective have they been?
- ✓ How does feedback from others influence your mindset and approach to challenges?

Journaling Prompts:

- ✓ Reflect on a challenge you faced recently. How did your mindset affect the outcome?
- ✓ Write about a time when you learned from criticism. How did this experience help you grow?
- ✓ List ways you can embrace challenges and view them as opportunities for growth.
- ✓ Create affirmations that can help shift your mindset from fixed to growth. How will you incorporate these into your daily routine?

Building a Support System

In the journey of overcoming failure and achieving success, having a strong support system is invaluable. Support systems provide emotional encouragement, practical advice, and a sense of belonging that can help us navigate through challenges. This chapter explores the power of a strong network, strategies for building and maintaining supportive relationships, and offers an action plan to create your own support system.

The Power of a Strong Network

The significance of a support system cannot be overstated. When facing failures and setbacks, having people who believe in you and offer encouragement can make a world of difference. A robust support system can provide different perspectives, share resources, and help you stay motivated during difficult times.

How Support Systems Contribute to Overcoming Failure

Support systems act as a safety net, cushioning the impact of failure and helping you bounce back more quickly. When you face setbacks, your network can provide the emotional support needed to maintain your confidence and self-esteem. They can remind you of your strengths and past achievements, helping you regain a positive outlook.

Additionally, support systems can offer practical advice and resources. Whether it's brainstorming solutions to a problem, providing mentorship, or offering a fresh perspective, the insights from your network can be crucial in overcoming obstacles. For instance, if you're struggling with a professional setback, a mentor with more experience can provide guidance on how to navigate the situation and suggest actionable steps to take.

Types of Support Systems

Support systems can take various forms, each playing a unique role in your life. Understanding the different types can help you build a comprehensive network that meets your diverse needs.

- ✓ **Family:** Family members often form the core of your support system. They provide unconditional love, emotional support, and a sense of belonging. During times of failure, family can offer a stable foundation to help you regain your footing.
- ✓ **Friends:** Friends provide companionship, understanding, and empathy. They can offer a listening ear, share their own experiences, and provide comfort during difficult times. Friendships can also offer practical support, such as helping you network or providing assistance with tasks.
- ✓ **Mentors:** Mentors are individuals with more experience and wisdom in a particular area. They can offer guidance, advice, and a broader perspective on challenges you face. A mentor can help you develop new skills, set realistic goals, and navigate your professional journey.
- ✓ **Professional Networks:** Colleagues, industry groups, and professional organizations can offer valuable support in your career. These networks provide opportunities for learning, collaboration, and growth. They can also help you stay updated on industry trends and connect with potential opportunities.

Finding and Building Your Support Network

Building a strong support network requires intentional effort and nurturing. It involves identifying people who can provide meaningful support and cultivating relationships based on mutual respect and trust.

Strategies for Identifying and Nurturing Supportive Relationships

- ✓ **Assess Your Current Network:** Start by evaluating your existing relationships. Identify individuals who have been supportive and consider how you can strengthen these connections. Also, identify gaps in your support system and think about who you can reach out to fill these gaps.
- ✓ **Be Proactive in Building Relationships:** Building a support network takes time and effort. Be proactive in reaching out to potential mentors, joining professional groups, and connecting with like-minded individuals. Attend networking events, participate in community activities, and leverage social media to build connections.
- ✓ **Foster Mutual Support:** Supportive relationships are built on mutual respect and reciprocity. Offer your support to others, whether it's through sharing resources, providing a listening ear, or offering assistance. This mutual exchange strengthens bonds and builds trust.
- ✓ **Communicate Openly and Honestly:** Open and honest communication is crucial in nurturing supportive relationships. Share your challenges, successes, and goals with your network. Be receptive to feedback and willing to share your own insights and experiences.

- ✓ **Show Appreciation:** Express gratitude to those who support you. Acknowledging their help and showing appreciation strengthens relationships and encourages continued support.

Case Studies of Effective Support Networks

- ✓ **Case Study 1: Sheryl Sandberg**
  Sheryl Sandberg, COO of Facebook, often speaks about the importance of having a strong support system in her professional journey. After facing personal tragedy with the sudden death of her husband, Sandberg relied heavily on her support network, which included family, friends, and colleagues. This network provided her with emotional strength, practical assistance, and professional guidance, enabling her to continue her career and advocate for women's leadership through her Lean In movement.
- ✓ **Case Study 2: Howard Schultz**
  Howard Schultz, former CEO of Starbucks, attributes much of his success to his strong support network. Growing up in a low-income family, Schultz faced numerous challenges. However, he found mentors who believed in him and provided guidance. These mentors helped him navigate the corporate world, develop leadership skills, and ultimately transform Starbucks into a global brand.

Action Plan: Creating Your Support System

Creating a strong support system involves intentional steps to build, nurture, and maintain relationships that can provide the encouragement and resources you need.

Steps to Build and Maintain a Strong Support Network

- ✓ **Identify Key Supporters:** List the people in your life who have been supportive. Consider family, friends, colleagues, and mentors. Identify any gaps in your network and think about how to fill them.
- ✓ **Reach Out and Connect:** Make an effort to connect with potential supporters. Schedule regular check-ins with existing supporters, attend networking events, and join groups or organizations that align with your interests and goals.
- ✓ **Nurture Relationships:** Build trust and rapport with your network by being supportive, showing appreciation, and maintaining open communication. Offer your help and be willing to listen and provide feedback.
- ✓ **Leverage Technology:** Use technology to stay connected with your support network. Social media, email, and messaging apps can help you maintain regular communication, even with those who are geographically distant.
- ✓ **Create a Support System Plan:** Develop a plan to regularly engage with your support network. Schedule regular meet-ups, phone calls, or virtual meetings. Keep track of your interactions and make notes on how you can offer support in return.

Tips for Asking for and Offering Support

Asking for Support:

- ✓ **Be Clear and Specific:** When asking for support, be clear about what you need. Whether it's advice, feedback, or assistance, being specific helps others understand how they can help.

- ✓ **Be Respectful of Their Time:** Acknowledge that everyone has their own commitments and be considerate of their time. Request support in a way that is convenient for them.
- ✓ **Express Gratitude:** Show appreciation for any support you receive. A simple thank you can go a long way in strengthening your relationship.

Offering Support:

- ✓ **Be Available and Attentive:** Make yourself available to support others. Listen attentively and provide thoughtful feedback or assistance.
- ✓ **Share Your Resources:** Offer resources, knowledge, or connections that may be helpful to others. Sharing what you have can strengthen your network.
- ✓ **Follow Through:** If you commit to providing support, ensure you follow through. Reliability builds trust and solidifies relationships.

Example Action Plan for Creating Your Support System

- ✓ **Monthly Networking Goal:** Set a goal to attend at least one networking event or join a new group each month. This helps you continuously expand your support network.
- ✓ **Weekly Check-Ins:** Schedule weekly check-ins with key supporters in your network. These can be casual catch-ups, professional meetings, or virtual hangouts.
- ✓ **Support Exchange:** Create a support exchange system where you regularly offer assistance to your network and ask for

support in return. This reciprocal approach ensures balanced and mutually beneficial relationships.

- ✓ **Appreciation Ritual:** Develop a ritual of expressing gratitude. This could be writing thank-you notes, giving small tokens of appreciation, or publicly acknowledging support on social media.

By following this action plan and nurturing your relationships, you can build a robust support system that helps you navigate failures, celebrate successes, and achieve your goals. Remember, a strong network is not just about having people around you, but about building meaningful connections that provide mutual support and encouragement.

Reflective Questions:

- ✓ Who are the key people in your support system, and how do they help you overcome failures?
- ✓ How do you identify and nurture supportive relationships in your life?
- ✓ Reflect on a time when someone in your support system helped you through a difficult period. What did they do that was most helpful?
- ✓ How can you be a better support for others in your network?

Journaling Prompts:

- ✓ Write about a time when your support system played a crucial role in helping you overcome a failure. What did you learn from this experience?

- ✓ Reflect on the different types of support systems (family, friends, mentors) in your life. How does each type contribute to your well-being and success?
- ✓ Create a plan to strengthen your support network. Who do you need to reach out to, and how will you build these relationships?
- ✓ How can you offer support to others in a meaningful way? Describe specific actions you can take.

Learning from Others

Learning from others is an invaluable strategy for navigating failure and moving towards success. The experiences, insights, and support of mentors, peers, and role models can provide guidance, inspiration, and practical advice. This chapter delves into the value of mentorship, the importance of peer support and role models, and offers an actionable plan to seek guidance and learn from others.

The Value of Mentorship

Mentorship is a powerful tool for personal and professional development. A mentor can provide wisdom, guidance, and support, helping you navigate through challenges and failures. The right mentor can offer a fresh perspective, share their experiences, and provide valuable advice on how to move forward.

How Mentors Can Guide You Through Failure

Mentors can help you see failure in a new light. They can share their own experiences of failure and how they overcame it, providing you with strategies and insights that you might not have considered. For example, consider the story of Oprah Winfrey. She faced significant setbacks early in her career, including being fired from her first television job. However, with the guidance and support of mentors, she was able to learn from these experiences, refine her skills, and eventually build a media empire.

Mentors can also help you identify and develop your strengths. They can provide constructive feedback, help you set realistic goals, and offer support as you work towards these goals. This guidance can be crucial in helping you build resilience, stay motivated, and achieve success.

Finding the Right Mentor for Your Needs

Finding the right mentor involves identifying someone whose experiences, values, and expertise align with your own goals and challenges. Here are some steps to help you find the right mentor:

- ✓ **Identify Your Goals and Needs:** Before seeking a mentor, clearly define your goals and what you hope to gain from the mentorship. Understanding your needs will help you identify the right person to guide you.
- ✓ **Look for Role Models:** Identify individuals in your field or area of interest who have achieved success and whom you admire. Look for people whose career paths or personal journeys resonate with you.
- ✓ **Seek Recommendations:** Ask colleagues, friends, or professional networks for recommendations. They might know someone who would be a good fit for you.
- ✓ **Do Your Research:** Once you have identified potential mentors, research their background, achievements, and values. Ensure they align with what you are looking for in a mentor.
- ✓ **Reach Out:** Approach potential mentors with a clear and respectful request. Explain why you admire them, what you hope to learn, and how you believe they can help you. Be specific about what you are asking for, whether it's regular meetings, occasional advice, or guidance on a particular project.

Learning from Peers and Role Models

While mentors provide one-on-one guidance, peers and role models also play a crucial role in your growth and development. Peers can offer support, share experiences, and provide a sense of camaraderie, while role models can inspire and motivate you to achieve your goals.

The Importance of Peer Support and Role Models

Peers can offer valuable insights and feedback based on their own experiences. They can provide support and encouragement during challenging times, and help you stay accountable to your goals. For instance, joining a peer support group or a professional association can connect you with like-minded individuals who share similar challenges and aspirations. These connections can provide a sense of community and mutual support.

Role models, on the other hand, can inspire you by demonstrating what is possible. Seeing someone who has achieved success despite facing similar challenges can motivate you to persevere and reach your own goals. For example, Steve Jobs, co-founder of Apple, faced numerous setbacks, including being ousted from the company he helped create. However, his resilience and eventual return to Apple, where he led the company to unprecedented success, serve as a powerful example of overcoming failure.

Examples of Successful Mentor-Mentee Relationships

One notable example of a successful mentor-mentee relationship is that of Maya Angelou and Oprah Winfrey. Maya Angelou served as a mentor to Oprah, offering guidance, wisdom, and support throughout her career. Oprah has often spoken about the profound impact Angelou had on her life, helping her navigate challenges and stay true to her values.

Another example is that of Bill Gates and Warren Buffett. Buffett has served as a mentor to Gates, providing invaluable advice on philanthropy and business. Their relationship has been marked by mutual respect and a shared commitment to making a positive impact on the world.

Action Plan: Seeking Guidance

Creating a support system of mentors, peers, and role models involves intentional steps to build and maintain these relationships. This action plan provides practical activities to help you seek guidance and learn from others.

Tips for Finding and Approaching Mentors

- ✓ **Clarify Your Objectives:** Clearly define what you hope to achieve through mentorship. This clarity will help you identify the right mentor and communicate your needs effectively.
- ✓ **Identify Potential Mentors:** Look for individuals whose experiences and achievements align with your goals. Use your network, professional associations, and online platforms to identify potential mentors.
- ✓ **Prepare Your Approach:** When reaching out to potential mentors, be respectful and specific. Explain why you admire them, what you hope to learn, and how you believe they can help you. Offer to meet at their convenience and be prepared to make a strong case for why you would benefit from their guidance.
- ✓ **Build the Relationship:** Once you have established a mentorship, nurture the relationship by being respectful of their time, being open to feedback, and showing

appreciation for their guidance. Regularly check in and update them on your progress.

Activities to Learn from Peers and Role Models

- ✓ **Join Professional Groups:** Participate in professional associations, online forums, or local meetups related to your field. These groups provide opportunities to connect with peers, share experiences, and gain insights.
- ✓ **Peer Learning Circles:** Form a peer learning circle with individuals who share similar goals. Meet regularly to discuss challenges, share resources, and provide support. This collaborative approach can enhance your learning and growth.
- ✓ **Role Model Research:** Identify role models who inspire you and study their journeys. Read their biographies, watch interviews, and analyze how they overcame challenges. Reflect on how you can apply their strategies to your own situation.
- ✓ **Shadowing and Observation:** If possible, shadow a mentor or role model in their work environment. Observing their behavior, decision-making processes, and interactions can provide valuable insights and learning opportunities.

Example Action Plan for Seeking Guidance

- ✓ **Monthly Mentor Meetings:** Schedule monthly meetings with your mentor to discuss your progress, challenges, and goals. Prepare an agenda for each meeting to ensure productive and focused discussions.
- ✓ **Peer Support Group:** Join or form a peer support group that meets bi-weekly. Use these

meetings to share experiences, seek advice, and provide mutual support.

- ✓ **Role Model Analysis:** Select one role model each month to study in depth. Read their books, watch their interviews, and take notes on key lessons and strategies. Reflect on how you can apply these lessons to your own journey.
- ✓ **Mentorship Feedback Loop:** Create a feedback loop with your mentor where you regularly update them on your progress and seek their input. This ongoing dialogue helps you stay accountable and make informed decisions.

By actively seeking guidance from mentors, peers, and role models, you can gain valuable insights, build resilience, and achieve your goals. Remember, learning from others is not just about receiving advice but also about building meaningful relationships that support your growth and success. Through intentional effort and nurturing these relationships, you can create a strong support system that helps you navigate failures and move towards success.

Reflective Questions:

- ✓ How have mentors influenced your personal and professional growth?
- ✓ What qualities do you look for in a mentor, and why are these important to you?
- ✓ Reflect on a peer or role model who has inspired you. What lessons have you learned from them?

- ✓ How can you apply the lessons learned from your mentors and role models to your own journey?

Journaling Prompts:

- ✓ Write about a mentor who has had a significant impact on your life. What specific advice or support did they provide?
- ✓ Reflect on a time when you learned something valuable from a peer. How did this experience shape your perspective?
- ✓ Create a plan to find and approach a potential mentor. What steps will you take, and what do you hope to achieve through this relationship?
- ✓ How can you become a mentor to someone else? Describe the actions you will take to support and guide others.

Developing New Skills

Developing new skills is a vital component of transforming failure into success. By identifying and addressing skill gaps, you can turn setbacks into opportunities for growth and improvement. This chapter explores how to assess the skills you need to develop, provides resources for learning and improvement, and offers a detailed action plan for creating and tracking your personalized skill development journey.

Identifying Skill Gaps

Understanding your current skill set and identifying gaps is the first step toward effective skill development. This process involves self-assessment, seeking feedback from others, and using specific tools to pinpoint areas that require improvement.

How to Assess the Skills You Need to Develop

- ✓ Self-assessment is a powerful tool for identifying skill gaps. Start by reflecting on your recent failures or setbacks. Consider the specific skills that, if improved, could have led to a different outcome. For example, if a project failed because of poor time management, you might need to develop better organizational and time management skills.
- ✓ Another approach is to set clear goals and determine the skills required to achieve them. Break down your goals into smaller tasks and identify the skills needed for each task. This method can help you see where your current abilities align with your goals and where gaps exist.

Tools for Skill Gap Analysis

Using structured tools can provide a more objective assessment of your skills. One effective method is the Skill Gap Analysis, which involves the following steps:

- ✓ List Required Skills: Identify the skills necessary for your desired role or goal. This could include technical skills, soft skills, or specific competencies relevant to your field.
- ✓ Assess Current Skills: Rate your proficiency in each of the required skills. Be honest with yourself and consider using a scale from 1 to 5, where 1 indicates no proficiency and 5 indicates expert-level proficiency.
- ✓ Identify Gaps: Compare your current skill levels with the required levels. Highlight the areas where there is a significant difference.
- ✓ Another useful tool is the Feedback Analysis, where you seek input from colleagues, mentors, or supervisors. Ask for constructive feedback on your performance and specific areas where you can improve. This external perspective can provide valuable insights that you might overlook.

Learning and Improving Skills

Once you have identified your skill gaps, the next step is to actively work on developing and improving those skills. Embracing a mindset of continuous learning is essential for overcoming failure and achieving long-term success.

Resources for Skill Development

There are numerous resources available to help you develop new skills. Here are a few options to consider:

- ✓ Online Courses: Platforms like Coursera, Udemy, and LinkedIn Learning offer a wide range of courses on various topics. These courses are often flexible, allowing you to learn at your own pace.
- ✓ Workshops and Seminars: Attending workshops and seminars can provide hands-on experience and networking opportunities. Look for events related to your field or areas of interest.
- ✓ Books and Articles: Reading books, articles, and research papers can deepen your knowledge and provide new perspectives. Choose materials that are well-regarded in your industry.
- ✓ Mentorship and Coaching: Working with a mentor or coach can provide personalized guidance and feedback. They can help you develop specific skills and offer support as you progress.
- ✓ Practice and Application: Practical experience is crucial for skill development. Seek opportunities to apply new skills in real-world situations, whether through projects, volunteering, or job assignments.

The Role of Continuous Learning in Overcoming Failure

Continuous learning is the process of constantly seeking to improve and expand your skill set. It involves staying curious, being open to new ideas, and embracing change. This mindset is particularly important when overcoming failure, as it allows you to adapt and grow from your experiences.

For example, consider the story of Richard Branson, the founder of the Virgin Group. Branson has faced numerous business failures, including the collapse of Virgin Cola and Virgin Megastores. However, his commitment to continuous learning and willingness to take risks have allowed him to build a diverse and successful business empire. Branson often attributes his success to his ability to learn from failures and persistently seek new opportunities for growth.

Action Plan: Skill Development Plan

Creating a personalized skill development plan is a structured approach to learning and improving new skills. This plan should be detailed, actionable, and include specific steps to track your progress.

Creating a Personalized Learning Plan

- ✓ Set Clear Objectives: Start by defining your learning objectives. What specific skills do you want to develop? Be as precise as possible. For example, instead of saying "improve communication skills," specify "enhance public speaking abilities."
- ✓ Identify Resources: List the resources you will use to develop these skills. This could include online courses, books, workshops, or mentorship. For each resource, note down the key topics covered and the time commitment required.
- ✓ Create a Timeline: Develop a timeline for your learning plan. Set realistic deadlines for completing each resource or achieving specific milestones. Break down your goals into manageable steps and allocate time each week to work on them.
- ✓ Develop a Routine: Establish a consistent learning routine. Dedicate specific times during the week to focus on skill development. Consistency is key to making steady progress.

Tracking Progress and Celebrating Milestones

Tracking your progress helps you stay motivated and identify areas where you need to adjust your plan. Here are some strategies to help you track and celebrate your achievements:

- ✓ Use a Learning Journal: Keep a journal to document your learning journey. Write down key takeaways, insights, and reflections after each learning session. This practice helps reinforce your learning and provides a record of your progress.
- ✓ Set Milestones: Break your learning goals into smaller milestones. For example, if your goal is to complete a certification course, set milestones for finishing each module. Celebrate each milestone to stay motivated.
- ✓ Seek Feedback: Regularly seek feedback from mentors, peers, or coaches. They can provide valuable insights and help you stay on track. Use their feedback to refine your learning plan and address any challenges.
- ✓ Reflect on Your Growth: Periodically review your learning journal and reflect on your progress. Acknowledge the skills you have developed and the improvements you have made. This reflection helps you appreciate your growth and stay committed to continuous learning.
- ✓ Reward Yourself: Celebrate your achievements, no matter how small. Rewards can be simple, such as taking a break, treating yourself to something you enjoy, or sharing your success with others. Celebrating your progress reinforces positive behavior and keeps you motivated.

Example Skill Development Plan

1. Objective: Improve Public Speaking Skills
   - ✓ Set Objectives:
   - ✓ Enhance ability to deliver engaging presentations.
   - ✓ Increase confidence in speaking to large audiences.
2. Identify Resources:
   - ✓ Enroll in an online public speaking course on Coursera.
   - ✓ Read "Talk Like TED" by Carmine Gallo.
   - ✓ Attend a local Toastmasters club.
3. Create a Timeline:
   - ✓ Complete the online course within three months.
   - ✓ Read the book within one month.
   - ✓ Attend Toastmasters meetings weekly for six months.
4. Develop a Routine:
   - ✓ Dedicate two hours every Saturday to the online course.
   - ✓ Read for 30 minutes each evening.
   - ✓ Attend Toastmasters meetings every Tuesday evening.
5. Track Progress:
   - ✓ Keep a learning journal to document key takeaways and reflections.
   - ✓ Set milestones for completing each module of the course.
   - ✓ Seek feedback from Toastmasters peers after each speech.
6. Reflect and Reward:
   - ✓ Review the learning journal monthly.
   - ✓ Celebrate completing the online course with a small reward.

- ✓ Share progress and achievements with a mentor for additional feedback.

By following this detailed action plan, you can systematically develop new skills, track your progress, and celebrate your achievements. Remember, skill development is a continuous process that requires dedication, persistence, and a willingness to learn from both successes and failures. Through intentional effort and the right resources, you can turn failures into opportunities for growth and success.

Reflective Questions:

- ✓ What skills do you feel you need to develop to overcome your current challenges?
- ✓ How do you typically approach learning new skills, and how effective has this been?
- ✓ Reflect on a time when you successfully learned a new skill. What methods and resources did you use?
- ✓ How can continuous learning help you move forward from failure and achieve success?

Journaling Prompts:

- ✓ Write about a skill gap you have identified. How will developing this skill help you in your personal or professional life?
- ✓ Reflect on the resources you have used in the past for skill development. Which ones were most effective, and why?
- ✓ Create a personalized learning plan for a specific skill you want to develop. Outline the steps you will take and the resources you will use.

- ✓ How will you track your progress and celebrate milestones in your skill development journey?

Taking Action

Taking action is the crucial step that bridges the gap between planning and achieving your goals. No matter how well you prepare, without execution, your plans remain mere ideas. This chapter delves into the importance of taking action, overcoming barriers like procrastination and fear of failure, and provides effective strategies to help you take decisive steps toward your goals. By the end of this chapter, you'll have a detailed, actionable plan to start implementing changes in your life.

From Planning to Execution

It's often said that the road to hell is paved with good intentions. This saying underscores the critical importance of moving from the planning stage to execution. While planning is necessary, action is what ultimately leads to change and success.

The Importance of Taking Action and Making Changes

Taking action transforms your plans into tangible results. It's the difference between knowing what needs to be done and actually doing it. Action is the catalyst that converts goals into reality, dreams into achievements, and aspirations into milestones. Without action, even the most meticulously crafted plans remain stagnant, and progress halts.

Consider the story of Sara Blakely, the founder of Spanx. Blakely had an idea for a new type of hosiery, but it was her determination to take action that turned Spanx into a billion-dollar company. She faced numerous rejections and setbacks, but her unwavering commitment to execution—cold-calling manufacturers, pitching to investors, and relentlessly improving her product—was key to her success.

Overcoming Procrastination and Fear of Failure

Procrastination and fear of failure are common barriers to taking action. Procrastination often stems from a fear of failure or a lack of confidence in one's abilities. To overcome these barriers, it's essential to address their root causes and implement strategies to move forward.

Start by understanding that failure is a natural part of the journey to success. Embrace failure as a learning opportunity rather than a setback. Break down your tasks into smaller, manageable steps to reduce the feeling of being overwhelmed. Use techniques like the Pomodoro Technique—working in focused intervals of 25 minutes followed by short breaks—to maintain productivity and momentum.

Visualize your success and the positive outcomes of taking action. This mental imagery can boost your motivation and reduce anxiety. Additionally, hold yourself accountable by setting deadlines and sharing your goals with someone who can provide support and encouragement.

Effective Action Strategies

Effective action-taking involves more than just deciding to act. It requires strategic planning, time management, and prioritization. Implementing these strategies can help you take consistent, purposeful steps toward your goals.

Techniques for Effective Action-Taking

- ✓ Time management is a cornerstone of effective action-taking. Prioritize your tasks based on their importance and urgency. The Eisenhower Matrix is a useful tool for this, helping you categorize tasks into four quadrants: urgent and important, important but not urgent, urgent but not important, and neither urgent nor important. Focus on tasks in the first two categories to make significant progress.

- ✓ Another effective technique is the SMART goals framework, which ensures that your goals are Specific, Measurable, Achievable, Relevant, and Time-bound. This clarity helps you stay focused and motivated. For instance, instead of setting a vague goal like "improve my public speaking," a SMART goal would be "deliver a 10-minute presentation to my team within the next month."

Examples of Successful Action-Taking

- ✓ Consider the example of Elon Musk, the founder of SpaceX and Tesla. Musk's success is largely due to his relentless action-taking and ability to execute ambitious plans. When he founded SpaceX, he faced significant skepticism and numerous failures. However, his unwavering commitment to action—continuously testing, learning from failures, and iterating on designs—eventually led to groundbreaking achievements, such as the successful launch and landing of reusable rockets.
- ✓ Another inspiring example is J.K. Rowling, who faced numerous rejections before publishing the first Harry Potter book. Her perseverance and determination to take action despite repeated setbacks highlight the power of persistence and resilience in achieving success.

Action Plan: Executing Your Plan

To help you take effective action and stay on track, here is a detailed, step-by-step action plan. This plan includes exercises to overcome procrastination, techniques for effective time management, and tips for maintaining motivation and accountability.

Steps to Implement Your Action Plan

- ✓ Define Your Goals: Clearly articulate what you want to achieve. Ensure your goals are SMART: Specific, Measurable, Achievable, Relevant, and Time-bound.
- ✓ Break Down Tasks: Divide your goals into smaller, actionable tasks. Create a task list with specific, manageable steps.
- ✓ Prioritize Tasks: Use the Eisenhower Matrix to categorize and prioritize your tasks. Focus on completing tasks that are both urgent and important first.
- ✓ Set Deadlines: Establish deadlines for each task and goal. This creates a sense of urgency and helps you stay focused.
- ✓ Create a Schedule: Develop a daily or weekly schedule that allocates time for working on your tasks. Use techniques like the Pomodoro Technique to maintain productivity.
- ✓ Take Action: Start working on your tasks immediately. Avoid overthinking and perfectionism, which can lead to procrastination.

Tips for Staying Motivated and Accountable

- ✓ Visualize Success: Regularly visualize the successful completion of your goals. This can boost your motivation and reinforce your commitment.
- ✓ Track Progress: Keep a journal or use a project management tool to track your

progress. Celebrate small milestones to maintain momentum.

- ✓ Seek Support: Share your goals with a friend, mentor, or accountability partner. Regular check-ins can provide support, encouragement, and constructive feedback.
- ✓ Reflect and Adjust: Periodically review your progress and adjust your plan as needed. Be flexible and open to making changes based on what you learn along the way.
- ✓ Reward Yourself: Reward yourself for completing tasks and reaching milestones. This positive reinforcement can keep you motivated and focused.

Example Action Plan: Launching a Personal Blog

Goal: Launch a personal blog within three months

1. Define Your Goals:
   - ✓ Launch a personal blog focused on travel and lifestyle within three months.
   - ✓ Publish at least three blog posts by the launch date.
2. Break Down Tasks:
   - ✓ Research blogging platforms and choose one.
   - ✓ Purchase a domain name and set up hosting.
   - ✓ Design the blog layout and create essential pages (About, Contact).
   - ✓ Write and edit three blog posts.
   - ✓ Promote the blog on social media.
3. Prioritize Tasks:
   - ✓ Week 1: Research and choose a blogging platform.
   - ✓ Week 2: Purchase domain and set up hosting.
   - ✓ Week 3-4: Design blog layout and create essential pages.
   - ✓ Week 5-8: Write and edit blog posts.

- ✓ Week 9-10: Promote the blog on social media.

4. Set Deadlines:

- ✓ Complete platform research by the end of week 1.
- ✓ Purchase domain and hosting by the end of week 2.
- ✓ Finish blog design and pages by the end of week 4.
- ✓ Complete writing and editing posts by the end of week 8.
- ✓ Start promoting the blog by the end of week 10.

5. Create a Schedule:

- ✓ Dedicate 1 hour each evening to research and setup tasks during weeks 1-4.
- ✓ Allocate 2 hours on weekends for writing and editing during weeks 5-8.
- ✓ Spend 30 minutes daily on social media promotion during weeks 9-10.

Tips for Staying Motivated and Accountable:

- ✓ Visualize the blog's launch and the excitement of sharing your content with readers.
- ✓ Track progress using a project management tool or journal.
- ✓ Share your goal with a friend who can check in with you weekly.
- ✓ Reflect on your progress and adjust tasks if necessary.
- ✓ Reward yourself with a treat or a fun activity after each milestone.

By following this detailed action plan, you can move from planning to execution and turn your goals into reality. Remember, the key to success lies in consistent, purposeful action. Embrace the process, learn from each step, and celebrate your progress along the way.

Reflective Questions:

- ✓ How do you feel about taking action after planning? What obstacles typically prevent you from executing your plans?
- ✓ Reflect on a time when you successfully took action on a plan. What strategies did you use to stay focused and motivated?
- ✓ What are your main sources of procrastination, and how can you overcome them?
- ✓ How can effective time management and prioritization help you achieve your goals?

Journaling Prompts:

- ✓ Write about a plan you have created but not yet executed. What is holding you back, and how can you overcome these obstacles?
- ✓ Reflect on a time when you procrastinated. What were the consequences, and what did you learn from this experience?
- ✓ Create a detailed action plan for a current goal. Include specific steps, deadlines, and accountability measures.
- ✓ How will you stay motivated and accountable as you work towards your goals? Describe your strategies and support system.

Reflecting and Adapting

In the journey of learning from failure, one of the most crucial steps is the ability to reflect on experiences and adapt accordingly. This chapter delves into the cycle of continuous improvement, the importance of ongoing reflection, and the tools and strategies needed to adapt to new challenges. By embracing a mindset of continuous improvement, you can turn setbacks into stepping stones and ensure lasting success.

The Cycle of Continuous Improvement

Continuous improvement is a process that involves regularly reflecting on your experiences, identifying areas for enhancement, and making necessary adjustments. This cyclical approach helps you to learn from each step and continually refine your strategies.

The Importance of Ongoing Reflection and Adaptation

Ongoing reflection allows you to assess what is working and what isn't. It provides insight into your progress and highlights areas where adjustments are needed. This practice is not about dwelling on mistakes but rather about understanding them and using that knowledge to improve.

Consider the Japanese concept of Kaizen, which means "change for better" and embodies the idea of continuous improvement. Companies like Toyota have successfully implemented Kaizen to enhance their manufacturing processes, leading to increased efficiency and reduced waste. The same principles can be applied to personal growth, where small, incremental changes lead to significant improvements over time.

Tools for Continuous Improvement

Several tools can help facilitate the process of continuous improvement. The PDCA (Plan-Do-Check-Act) cycle is one such tool. It involves planning a change, implementing it, checking the results, and acting based on what you learn. This iterative process ensures that improvements are made systematically and sustainably.

Feedback loops are another essential tool. Seeking feedback from others provides an external perspective on your actions and outcomes. Constructive feedback can reveal blind spots and offer valuable suggestions for improvement. Regularly incorporating feedback into your reflection process ensures that you remain objective and open to growth.

Adapting to New Challenges

Life is unpredictable, and new challenges often arise when least expected. The ability to adapt to these challenges is a critical component of resilience and success. Flexibility and a willingness to change course when necessary can make the difference between stagnation and growth.

How to Remain Flexible and Adapt to New Situations

Adaptability requires a mindset that views change as an opportunity rather than a threat. Embracing uncertainty and being open to new experiences can help you navigate through challenges more effectively. One way to cultivate this mindset is by practicing mindfulness. Mindfulness encourages you to stay present and respond to situations with clarity and calmness, rather than reacting impulsively.

Consider the story of Malala Yousafzai, who faced unimaginable challenges after being attacked by the Taliban for advocating girls' education. Instead of succumbing to fear, Malala adapted to her new reality by continuing her activism on an even larger scale. Her resilience and adaptability have made her a global symbol of courage and education.

Stories of Successful Adaptation

History is replete with examples of individuals who successfully adapted to new challenges. Steve Jobs, after being ousted from Apple, founded NeXT and later returned to Apple to lead the company to unprecedented success. His ability to adapt and reinvent himself was key to his legacy.

Another example is Oprah Winfrey, who overcame numerous personal and professional challenges to become one of the most influential media personalities in the world. Her ability to adapt to changing circumstances and continuously improve her skills has been a cornerstone of her success.

Action Plan: Continuous Improvement

To help you integrate the principles of reflection and adaptation into your life, here is a detailed action plan. This plan includes exercises for regular reflection, strategies for adapting to new challenges, and steps to create a habit of lifelong learning and adaptation.

Exercises for Regular Reflection and Adjustment

- ✓ Daily Reflection Journal: At the end of each day, take 10-15 minutes to reflect on your experiences. Write about what went well, what didn’t, and what you learned. This practice helps you to internalize your experiences and identify patterns.

- ✓ Weekly Review: Set aside time each week to review your journal entries. Look for recurring themes or issues and consider how you can address them. This helps in identifying long-term trends and making informed adjustments.
- ✓ Monthly Feedback Session: Seek feedback from a trusted friend, mentor, or colleague once a month. Ask for honest opinions on your progress and areas for improvement. Use this feedback to make necessary changes and enhance your strategies.

Creating a Habit of Lifelong Learning and Adaptation

- ✓ Set Learning Goals: Continuously set new learning goals based on your reflections and feedback. This keeps you focused on growth and improvement. For instance, if you realize that you need to improve your communication skills, set a goal to take a public speaking course.
- ✓ Embrace New Experiences: Regularly push yourself out of your comfort zone by trying new activities or taking on new challenges. This builds your adaptability and resilience. For example, if you're comfortable in a specific role at work, volunteer for a project that requires a different skill set.
- ✓ Stay Informed: Keep up with industry trends and developments by reading books, attending seminars, and networking with professionals in your field. This ensures that you remain relevant and can quickly adapt to changes in your environment.

Example Action Plan: Continuous Improvement in Career Development

- ✓ Daily Reflection Journal: Spend 15 minutes each evening writing about your workday. Note what tasks you accomplished, what challenges you faced, and any feedback you received.
- ✓ Weekly Review: Every Friday, review your journal entries. Identify any patterns, such as recurring challenges or frequent feedback on specific skills. Plan how you will address these in the coming week.
- ✓ Monthly Feedback Session: Schedule a monthly meeting with your supervisor or mentor to discuss your progress. Use their feedback to adjust your goals and strategies.
- ✓ Set Learning Goals: Based on your reflections and feedback, set specific learning goals. For example, if you need to improve your project management skills, enroll in a relevant course or workshop.
- ✓ Embrace New Experiences: Take on new responsibilities or projects at work that challenge you to use different skills. For instance, if you're usually involved in technical tasks, volunteer for a project that requires client interaction.
- ✓ Stay Informed: Subscribe to industry journals, attend conferences, and participate in professional networks. Regularly update your knowledge and skills to remain adaptable to industry changes.

By following this action plan, you can create a cycle of continuous improvement that allows you to learn from your experiences, adapt to new challenges, and achieve lasting success. Reflecting on your journey and making strategic adjustments ensures that you remain on the path to growth and fulfillment.

Reflective Questions:

- ✓ How do you incorporate reflection and adaptation into your personal and professional life?
- ✓ Reflect on a time when you adapted to a new challenge. What steps did you take, and what was the outcome?
- ✓ How can continuous improvement help you achieve long-term success?
- ✓ What tools and methods do you use for regular reflection and adjustment?

Journaling Prompts:

- ✓ Write about a recent experience where reflection helped you improve or adapt. What insights did you gain?
- ✓ Reflect on a challenge you faced and how you adapted to it. What strategies did you use, and what was the result?
- ✓ Create a plan for regular reflection and continuous improvement. Outline the tools and methods you will use.
- ✓ How can you foster a habit of lifelong learning and adaptation? Describe specific actions you will take.

Celebrating Success

Celebrating success is an integral part of the journey from failure to triumph. It's not just about the grand victories, but also the small wins that pave the way. Recognizing and celebrating these achievements can significantly boost your morale, reinforce positive behavior, and sustain your momentum. In this chapter, we will explore the importance of celebrating success, techniques for effective celebration, and how to sustain long-term success. We will also provide a detailed action plan for recognizing and celebrating your milestones.

Recognizing Achievements

The Importance of Celebrating Small and Big Wins

Celebrating your achievements, both big and small, is crucial for several reasons. Firstly, it reinforces positive behavior. When you acknowledge your progress, you motivate yourself to continue striving towards your goals. Secondly, celebration provides a sense of closure and accomplishment, helping to alleviate the stress and hard work that went into achieving the goal.

Consider the story of J.K. Rowling. Before she became a household name, Rowling faced numerous rejections from publishers. Each small step—completing her manuscript, finding an agent, getting the first positive feedback—was a victory that kept her motivated. Celebrating these small wins helped her persevere through the tough times.

Techniques for Effective Celebration

There are various techniques to effectively celebrate your achievements. One approach is to establish a reward system. Set specific milestones for your goals and attach a reward to each milestone. For example, after completing a significant project at work, treat yourself to a weekend getaway.

Another effective technique is maintaining a gratitude journal. Each day, write down three things you are grateful for, including your achievements. This practice helps you focus on the positive aspects of your journey and recognize your progress.

Reflect on the story of Thomas Edison, who held over 1,000 patents. Edison celebrated every small victory in his experiments, which kept him motivated through countless failures. His ability to appreciate incremental progress was key to his ultimate success.

Sustaining Success

How to Maintain Momentum and Continue Growing

Sustaining success requires a continuous effort to maintain momentum and growth. One way to do this is by setting new, challenging goals once you achieve your current ones. This ensures that you are always working towards something, keeping your motivation high.

Another essential aspect is to remain adaptable and open to learning. Success is not a destination but a journey of constant growth and improvement. Embrace new challenges and opportunities for learning, just as Nelson Mandela did throughout his life. Despite achieving monumental success in ending apartheid, Mandela continued to advocate for peace and education, sustaining his impact.

Examples of Long-Term Success Stories

Consider the career of Serena Williams. After winning her first Grand Slam title, she didn't rest on her laurels. Instead, she continued to train, adapt, and push her limits, resulting in a career that spans over two decades with numerous titles. Her story exemplifies how maintaining momentum and continually setting new goals can sustain long-term success.

Action Plan: Celebrating Milestones

Steps to Recognize and Celebrate Your Achievements

- ✓ Set Clear Milestones: Define specific milestones for your goals. For example, if your goal is to run a marathon, set milestones such as completing a 5K, a 10K, and a half marathon.
- ✓ Create a Reward System: Attach a meaningful reward to each milestone. This could be something small like a favorite treat for completing a 5K, or something bigger like a weekend trip for finishing a half marathon.
- ✓ Maintain a Celebration Journal: Keep a journal where you document each milestone you achieve. Write about what you accomplished, how you feel, and how you celebrated. This practice not only helps in recognizing your achievements but also serves as a motivational tool to look back on your progress.

Ideas for Meaningful Celebrations

- ✓ Personal Rewards: Treat yourself to something you love. This could be a special meal, a spa day, or a new gadget you've been eyeing.
- ✓ Sharing with Others: Celebrate with friends and family. Share your achievements with your support network and let them join in your

celebration. This not only reinforces your success but also strengthens your relationships.

- ✓ Gratitude Practice: Incorporate gratitude into your celebrations. Take time to reflect on the journey, express gratitude for the support you received, and acknowledge the effort you put in. Writing thank-you notes to those who helped you can be a powerful way to celebrate and strengthen your connections.
- ✓ Reflection and Planning: Use your celebration as a moment to reflect on what you've learned and plan your next steps. This keeps you focused and motivated for future achievements.

Example Action Plan: Celebrating Career Milestones

- ✓ Setting Milestones: If your goal is to advance in your career, set milestones such as completing a certification, getting a promotion, or leading a major project.
- ✓ Reward System: Reward yourself for each milestone. For completing a certification, treat yourself to a special dinner. For getting a promotion, perhaps plan a short vacation.
- ✓ Celebration Journal: Keep a journal where you document each career milestone. Write about the skills you gained, the challenges you overcame, and how you celebrated your success.
- ✓ Sharing with Others: Celebrate your career milestones with your colleagues and mentors. Host a small gathering or a virtual celebration to share your success and gratitude.

- ✓ Gratitude Practice: Reflect on the support you received from mentors, colleagues, and family. Write thank-you notes or express your gratitude in person.
- ✓ Reflection and Planning: Use your celebration as a time to reflect on your career path, the skills you've acquired, and the goals you want to set next. Plan your next steps to continue growing in your career.

By following this action plan, you can ensure that each achievement is recognized and celebrated meaningfully. This not only reinforces positive behavior but also keeps you motivated and focused on your continuous journey of improvement and success. Celebrating your successes, no matter how small, is a powerful tool in building resilience and maintaining momentum towards your long-term goals.

Reflective Questions:

- ✓ How do you typically celebrate your achievements? What impact does this have on your motivation and well-being?
- ✓ Reflect on a recent success. How did you recognize and celebrate it?
- ✓ How can celebrating small wins help you maintain momentum towards your larger goals?
- ✓ What techniques can you use to create a meaningful and effective reward system?

Journaling Prompts:

- ✓ Write about a recent achievement and how you celebrated it. What did this celebration mean to you?

- ✓ Reflect on the importance of gratitude in recognizing your achievements. How do you express gratitude for your successes?
- ✓ List the small wins you have achieved in the past month. How can you celebrate these in a way that motivates you to keep going?
- ✓ Create a reward system for yourself. What rewards will you give yourself for reaching specific milestones?

Inspiring Others

Inspiring others through your experiences of failure and success is a profound way to give back and create a lasting impact. By sharing your story, you can offer hope and guidance to those facing similar challenges. Becoming a mentor allows you to directly support and guide others, fostering resilience and success in the next generation. This chapter delves into the power of storytelling, the role of mentorship, and provides an action plan for giving back to your community.

Sharing Your Story

The Power of Storytelling in Inspiring Others

Stories have an unparalleled ability to connect, motivate, and inspire. When you share your journey of overcoming failure, you provide a relatable narrative that others can draw strength from. Your story becomes a beacon of hope, showing that failure is not the end but a stepping stone to success. Consider the story of Oprah Winfrey. From a challenging childhood to becoming one of the most influential women in the world, Oprah's journey is a testament to the power of resilience and perseverance. By openly sharing her struggles and triumphs, she has inspired millions to overcome their obstacles and pursue their dreams.

How to Effectively Share Your Journey with Others

Effective storytelling involves authenticity and vulnerability. To truly inspire others, you must be willing to share not just your successes but also your failures, fears, and doubts. Here are some tips to help you share your story:

- ✓ Be Honest and Transparent: Authenticity is key. Share your experiences honestly, including the setbacks and the lessons learned. This authenticity will resonate with your audience and make your story more impactful.
- ✓ Focus on the Journey, Not Just the Destination: Highlight the process of overcoming failure rather than just the end result. This provides valuable insights and encouragement for others who are still on their journey.
- ✓ Use Relatable Examples: Incorporate specific examples and anecdotes that your audience can relate to. This makes your story more engaging and easier to connect with.
- ✓ End with a Message of Hope: Ensure your story leaves your audience with a message of hope and empowerment. Emphasize that failure is a part of the journey and that success is attainable with perseverance and resilience.

Becoming a Mentor

How to Support and Guide Others Through Their Failures

Mentorship is a powerful way to inspire and support others. As a mentor, you provide guidance, encouragement, and practical advice based on your own experiences. Here's how you can effectively mentor others:

- ✓ Build Trust and Rapport: Establish a strong, trusting relationship with your mentee. Be open, approachable, and empathetic, creating a safe space for them to share their struggles and aspirations.

- ✓ Share Your Experiences: Use your own experiences of failure and success to guide your mentee. Share the lessons you've learned and the strategies that helped you overcome challenges.
- ✓ Provide Practical Advice: Offer concrete, actionable advice tailored to your mentee's specific situation. Help them set realistic goals and develop a plan to achieve them.
- ✓ Encourage and Motivate: Be a source of encouragement and motivation. Celebrate their successes, no matter how small, and help them stay positive and focused on their goals.

Building a Legacy of Resilience and Success

By mentoring others, you not only help them succeed but also build a legacy of resilience and success. Your guidance can empower others to overcome their failures and achieve their dreams, creating a ripple effect of positivity and growth.

Consider the example of Nelson Mandela. After spending 27 years in prison, Mandela emerged not with bitterness, but with a commitment to reconciliation and mentorship. His guidance and leadership inspired a nation to overcome its divisions and work towards a common goal.

Action Plan: Giving Back

Ways to Inspire and Mentor Others

- ✓ Public Speaking and Workshops: Share your story through public speaking engagements and workshops. This allows you to reach a wider audience and provide inspiration and practical advice to many people at once.
- ✓ Writing and Blogging: Write articles, blogs, or even a book about your journey. This not only

allows you to share your story but also provides a permanent resource that others can refer to for guidance and inspiration.

- ✓ One-on-One Mentoring: Offer to mentor individuals who are struggling with failure or looking to achieve their goals. This can be done through formal mentorship programs or informally within your community or professional network.
- ✓ Community Involvement: Get involved in community organizations and initiatives that support personal and professional development. Volunteer your time and expertise to help others overcome their challenges and succeed.

Activities for Community Involvement and Support

- ✓ Volunteer at Local Organizations: Offer your skills and experience to local nonprofits, schools, or community centers. Lead workshops, give talks, or provide one-on-one mentoring to help individuals develop resilience and achieve their goals.
- ✓ Start a Support Group: Create a support group for individuals facing similar challenges. This provides a safe space for people to share their experiences, receive support, and learn from each other.
- ✓ Mentorship Programs: Establish or participate in mentorship programs within your professional network or community. Pairing experienced individuals with those seeking guidance can have a profound impact on both parties.

- ✓ Online Communities: Join or create online communities where you can share your story and offer support to a broader audience. Online platforms provide a unique opportunity to connect with and inspire people from around the world.

Example Action Plan: Giving Back Through Mentorship

- ✓ Identify Your Audience: Determine who you want to inspire and mentor. This could be young professionals, students, entrepreneurs, or individuals facing specific challenges.
- ✓ Share Your Story: Write a blog series about your journey, highlighting the key lessons you've learned. Share these articles on social media and relevant online communities.
- ✓ Host Workshops: Organize workshops or webinars on topics related to overcoming failure and building resilience. Partner with local organizations or use online platforms to reach a wider audience.
- ✓ Offer Mentorship: Join a mentorship program or offer to mentor individuals in your community or professional network. Set aside dedicated time each week for mentoring sessions.
- ✓ Engage in Community Service: Volunteer with organizations that align with your passions and expertise. Offer your skills to support their initiatives and help individuals in need.

By following this action plan, you can effectively inspire and mentor others, creating a positive impact that extends beyond your own journey. Sharing your story and supporting others not only helps them overcome their challenges but also enriches your own life, reinforcing your resilience and commitment to continuous growth.

Reflective Questions:

- ✓ How has sharing your story of overcoming failure impacted others?
- ✓ Reflect on a time when someone else's story inspired you. What elements of their story resonated with you the most?
- ✓ What qualities do you think are essential for becoming a good mentor?
- ✓ How can you create a legacy of resilience and success through mentoring others?

Journaling Prompts:

- ✓ Write about your journey of overcoming failure. How can sharing this story inspire others?
- ✓ Reflect on the people who have mentored or supported you. How have they influenced your path, and how can you pay this forward?
- ✓ Create a plan to become a mentor. Who can you support, and what steps will you take to offer guidance?
- ✓ How can you get involved in your community to support others facing challenges? Describe specific actions you can take.

Practical Tools and Resources Templates

Below are ready-to-use templates and checklists for each relevant chapter, designed to help readers implement the action plans discussed in the book. Each template and checklist is crafted to be practical, engaging, and easy to use.

Chapter 1: Understanding Failure

Failure Reflection Worksheet

1. Define the Failure:
   - ✓ Describe the situation where you experienced failure.
2. Initial Reactions:
   - ✓ How did you initially feel about the failure?
3. Learning Points:
   - ✓ What did you learn from this failure?
4. Future Improvements:
   - ✓ How can you apply this learning to future situations?

Checklist: Reframing Failure

☐ Identify a recent failure.

☐ Reflect on the emotions and thoughts associated with the failure.

☐ List at least three things you learned from the experience.

☐ Develop a plan to use these learnings in future endeavors.

Chapter 2: Analyzing Your Failures

Failure Analysis Worksheet

1. Describe the Failure:

- ✓ Write a detailed description of the failure event.

2. Root Cause Analysis:
   - ✓ What are the potential root causes? (Use tools like Fishbone Diagram or 5 Whys)
3. Lessons Learned:
   - ✓ Identify the key lessons learned from this analysis.
4. Action Steps:
   - ✓ List specific actions to take to avoid similar failures in the future.

Checklist: Conducting a Failure Analysis

- ☐ Document the failure event.
- ☐ Conduct a root cause analysis.
- ☐ Identify lessons learned.
- ☐ Create an action plan based on findings.

Chapter 3: Building Resilience

Resilience Building Plan

1. Identify Stressors:
   - ✓ List situations that challenge your resilience.
2. Resilience Strategies:
   - ✓ What strategies can you use to build resilience? (e.g., mindfulness, exercise)
3. Support Systems:
   - ✓ Identify people who can support you in building resilience.
4. Daily Practices:
   - ✓ Develop a daily routine to practice resilience-building activities.

Checklist: Strengthening Resilience

- ☐ Identify key stressors.
- ☐ Choose resilience-building strategies.
- ☐ Engage your support system.
- ☐ Implement daily resilience practices.

Chapter 4: Setting New Goals

Goal Setting Worksheet

1. Define Your Goal:
   - ✓ What is your specific goal?
2. SMART Criteria:
   - ✓ Ensure your goal is Specific, Measurable, Achievable, Relevant, and Time-bound.
3. Action Steps:
   - ✓ List the steps you need to take to achieve your goal.
4. Milestones:
   - ✓ Identify key milestones and deadlines.

Checklist: Goal Setting Workshop

- ☐ Define clear, specific goals.
- ☐ Apply the SMART criteria to each goal.
- ☐ Outline the action steps needed.
- ☐ Set milestones and deadlines.

Chapter 5: Embracing a Growth Mindset

Mindset Shift Worksheet

1. Identify Fixed Mindset Thoughts:
   - ✓ List common thoughts that reflect a fixed mindset.
2. Reframe to Growth Mindset:
   - ✓ How can you reframe these thoughts into a growth mindset?
3. Affirmations:
   - ✓ Write down positive affirmations to encourage a growth mindset.
4. Challenges and Learning:
   - ✓ Identify recent challenges and what you learned from them.

Checklist: Mindset Shift

- ☐ Recognize fixed mindset thoughts.

- ☐ Reframe these thoughts positively.
- ☐ Use daily affirmations.
- ☐ Reflect on recent challenges and lessons learned.

Chapter 6: Building a Support System

Support System Plan

1. Identify Current Support:
   - ✓ List the people who currently support you.
2. Potential Support Members:
   - ✓ Who else can you include in your support system?
3. Nurturing Relationships:
   - ✓ What actions can you take to strengthen these relationships?
4. Asking for Help:
   - ✓ Develop a plan for how and when to ask for support.

Checklist: Creating Your Support System

- ☐ Identify existing support members.
- ☐ Consider potential new members.
- ☐ Plan actions to nurture relationships.
- ☐ Develop a strategy for seeking support.

Chapter 7: Learning from Others

Mentorship Plan

1. Identify Your Needs:
   - ✓ What areas do you need guidance in?
2. Find a Mentor:
   - ✓ List potential mentors and why they would be a good fit.
3. Approach Plan:
   - ✓ How will you approach and ask for mentorship?
4. Learning from Peers:

- ✓ Identify peers who can offer support and what you can learn from them.

Checklist: Seeking Guidance

- ☐ Determine your mentorship needs.
- ☐ Identify potential mentors.
- ☐ Develop an approach plan.
- ☐ Engage with peers for mutual learning.

Chapter 8: Developing New Skills

Skill Development Plan

1. Identify Skill Gaps:
   - ✓ What skills do you need to develop?
2. Learning Resources:
   - ✓ List resources you can use (courses, books, workshops).
3. Action Steps:
   - ✓ Outline steps to acquire these skills.
4. Progress Tracking:
   - ✓ Develop a system to track your progress.

Checklist: Skill Development

- ☐ Conduct a skill gap analysis.
- ☐ Gather learning resources.
- ☐ Outline specific action steps.
- ☐ Implement a progress tracking system.

Chapter 9: Taking Action

Action Execution Plan

1. Define Actions:
   - ✓ What specific actions do you need to take?
2. Prioritize Actions:
   - ✓ Rank actions by priority.
3. Overcome Procrastination:
   - ✓ Identify and address reasons for procrastination.
4. Monitor Progress:

- ✓ How will you track your action steps and progress?

Checklist: Executing Your Plan

- ☐ List all necessary actions.
- ☐ Prioritize these actions.
- ☐ Develop strategies to overcome procrastination.
- ☐ Set up a progress monitoring system.

Chapter 10: Reflecting and Adapting

Continuous Improvement Plan

1. Reflection Schedule:
   - ✓ How often will you reflect on your progress?
2. Improvement Tools:
   - ✓ Identify tools and methods for reflection (PDCA, feedback loops).
3. Adapting Strategies:
   - ✓ Develop strategies for adapting to new challenges.
4. Continuous Learning:
   - ✓ Plan for ongoing learning and development.

Checklist: Continuous Improvement

- ☐ Schedule regular reflection periods.
- ☐ Select improvement tools.
- ☐ Create adapting strategies.
- ☐ Commit to continuous learning.

Chapter 11: Celebrating Success

Celebration Plan

1. Identify Achievements:
   - ✓ What achievements will you celebrate?
2. Celebration Methods:
   - ✓ How will you celebrate each achievement?
3. Gratitude Practices:
   - ✓ Develop practices for expressing gratitude.
4. Long-term Goals:

- ✓ How do these celebrations align with your long-term goals?

Checklist: Celebrating Milestones

- ☐ List your achievements.
- ☐ Decide on celebration methods.
- ☐ Implement gratitude practices.
- ☐ Align celebrations with long-term goals.

Chapter 12: Inspiring Others

Mentorship and Community Support Plan

1. Identify Stories:
   - ✓ What parts of your story will you share?
2. Find Mentees:
   - ✓ Who can you mentor?
3. Community Involvement:
   - ✓ Identify ways to support your community.
4. Legacy Building:
   - ✓ How will you build a legacy of resilience and success?

Checklist: Giving Back

- ☐ Identify key stories to share.
- ☐ Find potential mentees.
- ☐ Plan community involvement activities.
- ☐ Develop a legacy building strategy.

Conclusion

As we reach the end of **"Learning from Failure: *Keys to Success,"*** it's important to reflect on the journey we've undertaken together. This book has been a comprehensive exploration of the invaluable lessons failure can teach us and the paths we can take to turn setbacks into stepping stones towards success. Through understanding, analyzing, and embracing our failures, we can unlock new levels of personal and professional growth.

Throughout the chapters, we delved deep into the nature of failure, examining how it is perceived and how it impacts our lives. We learned that failure is not a definitive end but rather a pivotal part of the success journey. By reframing our mindset and viewing failure as an opportunity for learning and growth, we can transform our setbacks into powerful catalysts for change.

We have also emphasized the importance of building resilience, setting new goals, and cultivating a growth mindset. These elements are crucial in bouncing back from failure and ensuring that we are better prepared for future challenges. The stories of resilient individuals like Nelson Mandela and Malala Yousafzai have shown us that the human spirit is capable of incredible strength and perseverance.

One of the core themes of this book has been the value of support systems and mentorship. Surrounding ourselves with a strong network of family, friends, mentors, and peers can provide the encouragement and guidance needed to navigate difficult times. By sharing our experiences and learning from others, we can build a robust foundation for success.

The practical tools and resources provided, such as templates, worksheets, checklists, and action plans, are designed to help you implement the strategies discussed in this book. These tools are meant to be used and revisited as you continue your journey, ensuring that you stay on track and make continuous progress.

Reflective questions and journaling prompts at the end of each chapter have encouraged you to think deeply about your experiences and how you can apply the lessons learned. By engaging with these prompts, you have taken the time to internalize the concepts and make them a part of your daily life.

As you move forward, remember that success is not a destination but a continuous journey. Embrace each failure as a learning opportunity, remain resilient in the face of adversity, and keep setting new goals that challenge and inspire you. Celebrate your successes, no matter how small, and use them as motivation to keep pushing forward.

Most importantly, consider how you can inspire others by sharing your story and becoming a mentor. Your journey can serve as a beacon of hope and guidance for those who are struggling with their own failures. By giving back and supporting others, you create a legacy of resilience and success that extends beyond your own achievements.

Thank you for embarking on this journey with me. I hope that this book has provided you with valuable insights, practical tools, and the encouragement needed to turn your failures into keys to success.

Remember, you have the power to learn, grow, and thrive no matter what challenges you face.
With unwavering support and best wishes for your continued success,

About the Author
'GERARD ASSEY'

Gerard Assey is a Graduate in Economics, a PGD in Management (HRD) and holds a Doctorate in Leadership. Gerard holds several International Qualifications in Sales, Debt Collection, Training & Teaching, and is a 'Fellow' of the prestigious 'Institute of Sales & Marketing Management'-UK, a Certified NLP Practitioner, a 'Certified Trainer', an 'Accredited Management Teacher-Behavioral Sciences', a 'Certified Competency Facilitator', a 'Certified Management Consultant'- (the International credentials of a professional management consultant, awarded in accordance with global standards of the ICMCI); and a Certification from the University of Michigan in 'Successful Negotiation: Essential Strategies and Skills'

He is also a Member of the 'National Association of Sales Professionals' backed with several years experience in varied industries, both in India and Overseas. He also holds an 'Etiquette Consultant' Certification from the USA (by Sue Fox, Author of Best Seller: 'Business Etiquette for Dummies'. She has trained some of the top celebrities' world over). He was also a recipient of a scholarship for extensive training in Japan on 'Corporate Management for India'.

Gerard Assey is 'Founder & Chief Corporate Trainer' of the Group: '**Citius, Altius, Fortius Unlimited**'- an organization that **celebrated 20 years of Glorious Service** in 2021, focusing on 3 Core Competencies:

People. Performance. Profit; in functional areas of Sales & Marketing, HR & Organizational Development, covering Recruitment, Training & Consultancy!

Having managed organizations with large Sales Forces in India & Overseas, his specialization cover extensive areas of Sales Training (All levels - Presentation, Negotiation, Key/ Strategic Accounts Management & Managerial Skills for all sectors), Bid Proposal/ Capture Planning/ Management Trainings, Retail Sales, Customer Service & Customer Retention Programs, Training for Prevention & Collection of Debt, Self & Personal Development Programs (Time Management, Teamwork & Team Building, Business Etiquette & Personal Grooming, Leadership & Managerial Skills, People Management Skills, Train-the-Trainer etc), including preparation of Custom-designed Business Manuals for Internal (HR, Induction, and Sales etc) & External use (Instruction, User Manuals).

Gerard has successfully conducted over 6200 Trainings & Workshops (as of June '24) all across India, Middle East, Africa, Europe & S.E. Asia. Besides public programs conducted regularly, both in India & Overseas, he has some of the top names as clients whom he services from Single Owners to large Public & Government undertakings, covering all sectors, for their in-house needs.

His website: www.CollectionSkills.com is the only one in this part of the world to be featured in the 'Collections & Credit Risk Magazine-USA' under 'Who's Who in Training' and ranks TOP, along with other websites listed below on most search engines.

Gerard is author of 132 books already (June 2024)

A few of our business related books:

1. Bite-sized Bits on Commonsense Management
2. Heart to Heart on Life's Principles'
3. How to become a Successful Manager
4. The Sales Professionals' Master Workbook of S.Y.S.T.E.M.S
5. The Professional Business Email Etiquette Handbook & Guide
6. The Professional Business Video-Conferencing Etiquette Handbook & Guide
7. Professional Presentation Skills
8. Exceptional Customer Service
9. Professional Tele-Marketing Skills
10. Professional Debt Collection Skills
11. The G.R.E.A.T. Sales & Service Workbook
12. Sales Training Advantage for Results (*The Ultimate Sales Training Manual to enable you stand out as a S.T.A.R.*)
13. CEO Daily Planner & Organizer
14. The Sales Professionals' Master Daily Planner
15. The Professional Debt Collector's Master Daily Planner
16. My Daily Planner & Organizer
17. MY EMERGENCY INFORMATION RECORD (Family Emergency & Peace of Mind Planner)
18. The Ultimate Therapist & Counselors Planner and Organizer
19. Building an Ethical Workplace
20. Managing Relationships at Work
21. Managing Business Meetings Effectively
22. Effective Delegation Skills
23. Goal Setting for Success
24. B2B Selling by Email
25. Professional Business Etiquette & Grooming
26. Dining Etiquette & Table Manners
27. Effective Networking Skills
28. Grooming, Etiquette & Manners for Teens, Young Adults & Future Leaders
29. Inter-Personal Skills
30. Get Ready, Get Hired!
31. Selling in a Recession
32. Effective Receivables Management in an Economic Downturn!
33. Real Estate & Property Sales Training
34. Credit Sales & Accounts Receivable Management
35. Selling Skills for Real Estate & Property Advisors

36. Take G.R.E.A.T. C.A.R.E!
37. Spa, Salon & Health Club Selling Skills
38. Selling Travel, Holiday & MICE Services
39. Selling Skills for Spa's, Salons & Health Clubs
40. Retailing in Salons & Spas
41. Selling Holiday, Vacation, Tours & Packages
42. The Power of Sales Referrals
43. Selling Luxury
44. Technical Selling Skills
45. Financial Advisors Sales Training
46. Dealing with Burnout at Work Monopolize Your Markets
47. Selling to Affluent Customers
48. Growing up with Grace
49. Financial Selling Skills
50. *The Effective Manager's Guide: Key Skills to Thrive*
51. From Aspiring to Inspiring: A Guide for New Managers on the Rise
52. The Power of Focus
53. Selling with Integrity: Sell Like Jesus The Perfect Role Model!
54. 31 Habits of Champions: Your 31-Day Journey to Greatness
55. Rejecting Grasshopper Talk: From Grasshopper to Giant-Killer-*Defeating Giants Daily!*
56. Navigate the AI-Powered Future of Bid & Proposals: Up-Skill to Stay Relevant with Alternative Career Paths & Opportunities
57. Hiring Sales Winners
58. Present with Impact
59. Success Unlocked: *Breaking Free from Habits that Hold You Back*
60. Complaints to Cheers, Feedback to Gold: Mastering Complaints Management
61. Thriving Together: *Cultivating Diversity, Equity, and Inclusion*
62. Coaching Skills for Sales Managers
63. Soaring to Success in Business & Leadership: Swifter, Higher, Stronger!
64. From Classroom to Podium: A Student's Guide to Powerful Public Speaking & Presentation Skills
65. Developing Self-Discipline
66. The CEO's 31-Day Power Plan: Unlocking Success through Essential Traits
67. Credibility Matters

68. A Winning Attitude
69. Bid & Proposal Management Using AI
70. Sales Forecasting: A Practical & Proven Guide to Strategic Sales Forecasting
71. Elevate & Energize: *50 Dynamic & Fun Activities for Peak Workplace Morale*
72. 'Sales SOS! Sales on Fire! *30 Days to Conquer Chaos & the Nightmares of Success!'*
73. Mastering Sales Managerial Skills: *Building High-Performing Teams & Driving Exceptional Results*
74. Eagle-Eyed Leadership: Unleashing the Power of 31 Lessons from Eagles
75. The Ultimate Employee Training Guide: *Training Today, Leading Tomorrow*
76. Being More Accountable at Work
77. Creating a Culture of Continuous Improvement
78. Effective Questioning & Listening Skills
79. The Power of Value Selling
80. The Growth Mindset
81. Mastering Professional Help Desk Skills
82. The Power to Lead with Empathy
83. Being Prepared: The Key to Unlocking Success
84. Youthful Spark-Youth Energizers, Activities and Games-Igniting the Fun in Youth
85. Ignite your Motivation for Success
86. Elevate Your Executive Presence: *Your Roadmap to Executive Excellence*
87. Smart Decisions: *Mastering Problem Solving with Strategic Solutions for Business Success*
88. Strategic Planning: *Developing and Implementing Strategic Plans to Achieve Long-Term Business Goals*
89. The Power of Stay Interviews
90. Developing G.R.I.T.
91. Adaptability
92. Diagnosis- *A Key Skill for Leadership*
93. The Burnout-Proof Salesperson: *The Master Guide to Preventing Stress & Burnout*- Strategies for Thriving in Sales
94. Learning from Failure: *Keys to Success*

Besides regularly contributing to business & trade journals, including international ones such as the 'Creative Training Techniques' and the 'Sales News' of the U.S.A, He is also a member of several prestigious bodies & trade associations, having participated in many Conferences & Workshops in India & Overseas.

Prior to his last assignment of leading & managing a large MNC as head, Gerard had a 3-year stint in the Middle East as a Consultant with a leading British Consultancy Firm.

As the past 'Official Country Representative' for the International Business Award- 'THE STEVIES'-(the business world's own Oscar) for about 4 years- he ensured a few Indian companies that qualify for the same every year!

Gerard can be contacted at:
Email: training@Sales-Training.in,training@CollectionSkills.com
Websites:

www.Sales-Training.in
www.EtiquetteWorks.in
www.CollectionSkills.com
www.RetailSalesTraining.in
www.SalesTrainingIndia.com
www.ManualPreparation.com
www.TrainingWithPuppets.com
www.FirstContactAcademy.com
www.SalesAndMarketingRecruiter.com

Our TRAININGS that can help your team

- ✓ **Sales Effectiveness**: Selling Skills for any Sector: Service/ Logistics/ FMCG Realty/ Insurance & Finance/ Media/ SPA's, Health Clubs & Salons/ Key Account Management, Effective Negotiation Skills/ Bid & Proposal Management Skills/ Retail Sales Training: Any Sector (Auto, Jewelry, Clothing, Luxury etc)
- ✓ **Customer Service Skills**-Complaints Handling & Customer Retention
- ✓ **Debt Prevention & Collection Skills**
- ✓ **Etiquette & Grooming**
- ✓ **Leadership & Managerial Skills**
- ✓ **Self & Personal Development Skills**: Presentation Skills/ Effective Communication Skills/Business Proposal Writing Skills/ Problem Solving & Decision Making Skills/ Empowering Secretaries-The perfect PA! (For Secretaries & PA's)/ Effective Time Management/ Teamwork & Teambuilding/ P.R.I.D.E- **P**ersonal **R**esponsibility **I**n **D**elivering **E**xcellence

www.ingramcontent.com/pod-product-compliance
Lightning Source LLC
LaVergne TN
LVHW010114170826
845678LV00012B/2405

* 9 7 8 8 1 9 7 2 5 9 1 8 0 *